Kitchens and Baths

Publisher: **Paco Asensio**

Editor: **Haike Falkenberg**

Text: **Montse Zapata**

Translation: **Bill Bain (introduction), Matthew Clarke**

Graphic Design: **Mireia Casanovas Soley**

2002 © LOFT Publications
Domènech, 7-9 2 2. 08012 Barcelona. Spain
Tel.: +34 93 218 30 99
Fax: +34 93 237 00 60
loft@loftpublications.com
www.loftpublications.com

HBI ISBN: 0-06-008677-7
WG ISBN: 0-8230-2588-8

PRINTED IN SPAIN
I.G. FERRE OLSINA, S.A.

D.L.: 8460-2002

2002 © Loft Publications S.L. and HBI,
an imprint of HarperCollins International

First published in 2002 by LOFT and HBI,
an imprint of HarperCollins International
10 East 53rd St. New York, NY 10022-5299

Distributed in the U.S. and Canada by
Watson-Guptill Publications
770 Broadway New York, NY 10003-9595
Telephone: (800) 451-1741 or (732) 363-4511 in NJ, AK, HI Fax: (732) 363-0338

Distributed throughout the rest of the world by
HarperCollins International
10 East 53rd St. New York, NY 10022-5299
Fax: (212) 207-7654

If you would like to suggest projects for inclusion in our
next volumes, please e-mail details to us at:
loft@loftpublications.com

Kitchens and Baths

Baths

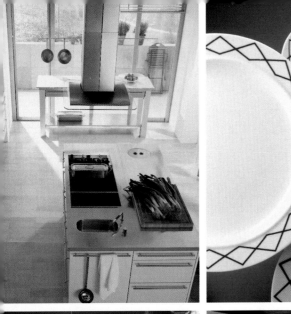
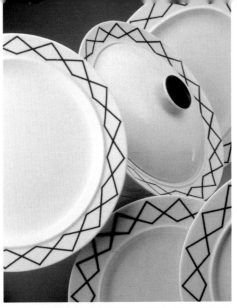

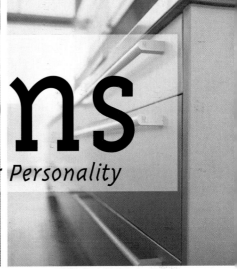
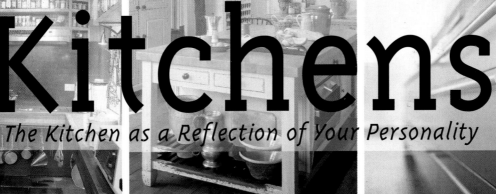

Kitchens

The Kitchen as a Reflection of Your Personality

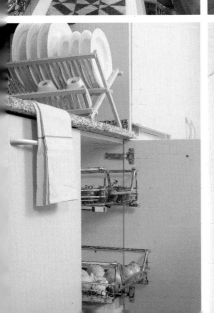

The kitchen is one of the rooms of the house where the greatest amount of technology is concentrated. Hence the constant development of new designs. More than one person will remember the old economical coal-burning stoves; the arrival at the end of the fifties of the most revolutionary fuel of the age, butane; and the "white line" ranges of the seventies. Until then, the kitchen was a family space, and in the next decade, it declined as the center of family get-togethers. The age of frozen foods and TV dinners had arrived, and the new aim was to prepare as little as possible.

But trends are cyclic, and after some years spent in the background, the kitchen again has a major role that even includes the luxury of opening into such noble spaces as the living room. Cutting-edge designs involve total integration of kitchen/dining room/living room. The kitchen now has pride of place and while it will always be a work space it has also taken on the trappings of a social area. Don't guests always end up in kitchen conversations? These days, they don't even have to move from the sofa to do so.

So, kitchen fittings now come in designs similar to those in the living room. They are simple. They are plain and they don't interfere with the beauty of the furniture. The materials tend to be wood, which is capable of carrying the space on its own; lacquered finishes, because the paints available have an infinite color

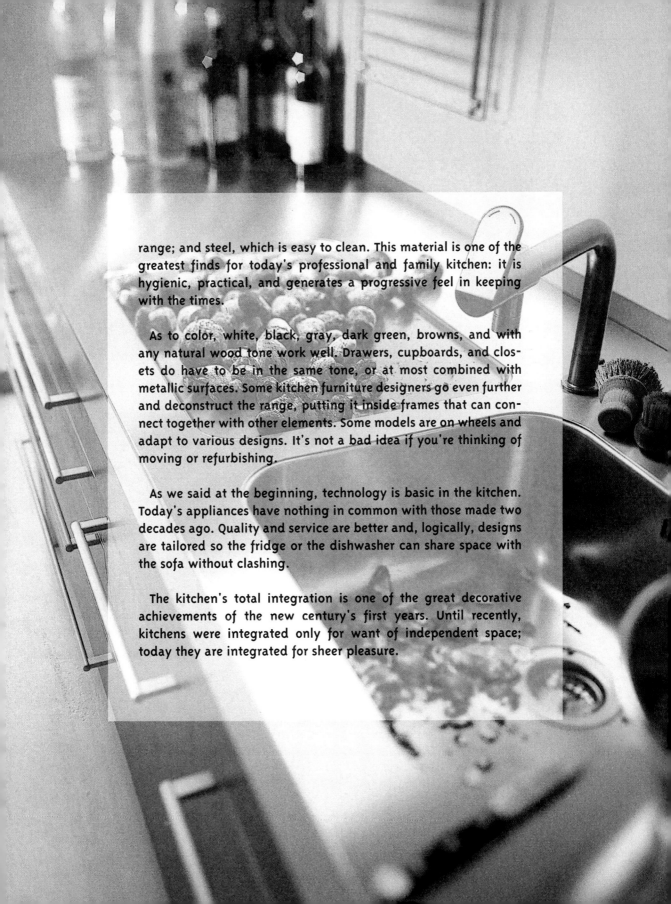

range; and steel, which is easy to clean. This material is one of the greatest finds for today's professional and family kitchen: it is hygienic, practical, and generates a progressive feel in keeping with the times.

As to color, white, black, gray, dark green, browns, and with any natural wood tone work well. Drawers, cupboards, and closets do have to be in the same tone, or at most combined with metallic surfaces. Some kitchen furniture designers go even further and deconstruct the range, putting it inside frames that can connect together with other elements. Some models are on wheels and adapt to various designs. It's not a bad idea if you're thinking of moving or refurbishing.

As we said at the beginning, technology is basic in the kitchen. Today's appliances have nothing in common with those made two decades ago. Quality and service are better and, logically, designs are tailored so the fridge or the dishwasher can share space with the sofa without clashing.

The kitchen's total integration is one of the great decorative achievements of the new century's first years. Until recently, kitchens were integrated only for want of independent space; today they are integrated for sheer pleasure.

Different Styles

Modern Kitchens
Minimalist Kitchens
Rustic Kitchens
Integrated Kitchens

Modern Kitchens

Modern kitchens with an avant-garde look usually utilize a single material and color. The main objectives are architectural integrity and minimalist style.

© Gene Raymond Ross

Today's modern or avant-garde kitchens are characterized by their restrained design. No moldings or handles disrupt the straight lines of the furniture, as if seeking to recapture the German-style kitchen that was so fashionable at the beginning of the nineties. These kitchens are usually monochrome, often white, or a subdued, neutral shade like gray or dark green. Their worktops and accessories are normally made of steel. Because of its industrial feel, steel is prevalent in many professional kitchens, and always looks good when combined with even the warmest of materials, such as wood. Apart from the aesthetic criteria that define the modern kitchen —the dominance of pure lines and simple designs— the fittings emphasize comfort. Not only are external features like faucets and electrical appliances finished down to the last detail, but the interior of every drawer and cabinet is designed to make it easier to arrange and find the utensils and foodstuffs stored inside them. This marks a gradual return to the traditional German kitchen, where high cabinets fitted with doors are indispensable.

© Gene Raymond Ross

Technology and innovative mechanisms have been skillfully used to organize the layout in this loft, where the kitchen has been completely integrated into the sitting room. A large table made of treated glass serves as a desktop, a dining table and a side table for the sitting room.

© Gene Raymond Ross

A mechanism makes it possible to raise or lower the tabletop to the required height and turn it up to 180 degrees by means of the axis supporting the weight of the structure.

© Gene Raymond Ross

The floor plan demonstrates how the table is the dominant feature and how the mechanism allows the surface to rotate up to 180 degrees.

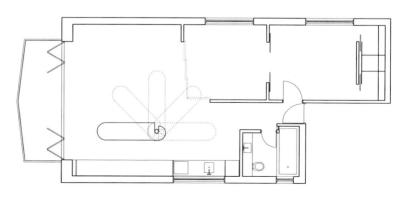

This kitchen, with its totally minimalist design, vaguely recalls an old country kitchen, with its basin set on a large worktop to wash the dishes and its free-standing stove with several burners. The structure is made of steel and concrete and all furniture has been strictly eliminated.

© Matteo Piazza

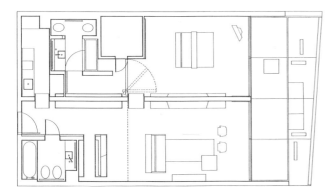

The areas of this residence are quite small, inspiring the use of cool and lightweight materials, like glass and steel, to create a more expansive atmosphere.

The glass roof, which is the floor of the upper floor, and porthole, inspired by a ship's cabin, let in sunlight both from above and from the side.

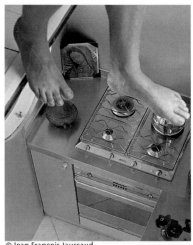

© Jean François Jaussaud

© Jean François Jaussaud

© Reiner Lautwein

The kitchen directly connects with the dining room, which also functions as an office.

The width and rectangular shape of the kitchen permitted the distribution of furniture along three surfaces: the two laterals attached to the walls and a central island into which a sink has been set also function as work surfaces.

Interior design by:
Claire Bataille & Paul Ibens

© Reiner Lautwein

© Reiner Lautwein

The kitchen is the only enclosed space inside the home and occupies the central zone of a large living expanse. This volume serves as a visual separation between the living and dining room areas.

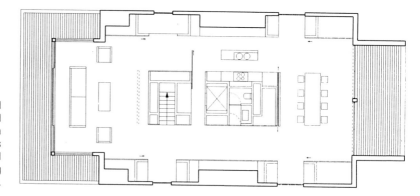

© Duccio Malagamba

The traditional high cabinets have been
replaced by shelves and independent drawer
units to take advantage of the space and
leave it more open.

The arrangement of the various spaces in
this rectangular house was determined by
the sources of sunlight.

The rectangular floors required inventive
solutions: in this case, the kitchen occupies a
volume perpendicular to the main floor,
allowing the house to receive far more
natural light.

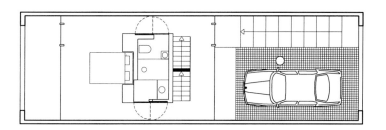

© Alan Williams

The splash of red makes the free-standing unit the undisputed star of this space and focuses attention on the kitchen area, with its simple white furnishings. Bright colors like red are always attractive in a space with natural light and architectural elements.

© Alan Williams

© David M. Joseph

The graphite-gray kitchen makes a
striking impact against the white walls
and floor of this large loft. The kitchen
has been adapted to the loft's
architectural features and is set
against the wall, like a fitted closet.
The steel worktop and cupboard
handles stand out against the furniture.

© David M. Joseph

Minimalist Kitchens

The basic tenets of minimalist design provide perfect solutions to the problems posed by rectangular, tube-shaped kitchens.

© Montse Garriga

Without a doubt, minimalist design, which is in vogue today, is the perfect solution for kitchens that are excessively long and narrow. The typical tube-shaped kitchen is no longer a problem and can even be very practical. The shape usually demands that all the furnishings and electrical appliances be set along one wall, so when the kitchen is in operation all movements are linear, either to the left or to the right. Why not enhance the feeling of a tube to create an innovative decoration? When choosing furniture, avoid any excessive trimmings, such as moldings, as well as any dark or very strong colors, as they stand out visually from the wall and can overwhelm a small workspace. It is best to choose furniture with smooth surfaces: decide on a single color and avoid mixing too many different kinds of materials. Another good idea is to attract attention to the floor: wood, slate and painted concrete are very striking options.

A long, tube-shaped space can be improved through an intelligent layout: the storage modules in this kitchen are only 14 inches deep.

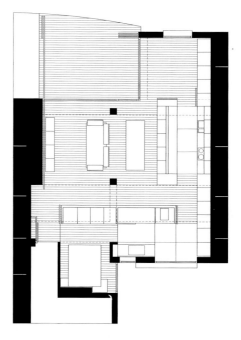

© César San Millán

A storage unit has been put in to separate the kitchen from the dining room; one side serves as a pantry, while the other side boasts a spacious closet for storing all the dishes, glassware and table linen. Since the unit does not go right up to the ceiling, it is not too overpowering.

© Eugeni Pons

© Eugeni Pons

© Eugeni Pons

The use of wood, even in small touch-es, adds warmth to kitchen furnishings and makes the space more cozy and inviting.

© Pere Planells

When the exterior views are worth seeing it is a good idea to reverse the layout of the kitchen. The work unit, with the stove and sink built in, is in the center to provide access from both sides. The pantry, refrigerator and oven are set against the side wall to avoid any interference with the central unit.

Rustic Kitchens

Natural materials like wood and stone set off by soft colors are the dominant features of a rustic kitchen.

© Ricardo Labougle

The rustic style is perhaps the only one that has remained untouched by the passing of time and the changing of fashions, as the rustic aesthetic is based on the colors and materials found in nature. Wood, in any of its forms, is the basic material for any kitchen with a country feel. Furthermore, rustic furniture design usually features molding or frames that set off doors; handles that are smaller and decorated; work surfaces that incorporate natural materials like granite and white marble; and walls that are painted or clad with wood or handmade tiles. High pieces of furniture are nearly always ruled out in favor of display shelves. The genuine rustic kitchen is a stone shell —although these days it is made of concrete— fitted with wood doors or some simple curtains. Sometimes the stonework is left exposed to emphasize the underlying natural spirit of the rustic kitchen. Even electrical appliances are left on display and stand free of the furniture.

© Undine Pröhl

This space is endowed with an abundance of natural light, and the beamed roof is very high, making it possible to equip and decorate the kitchen with various types of pale wood at no risk of overloading or darkening the setting. The woods used are ash, maple and pine.

© Undine Pröhl

The visible wooden plate racks, the double-tap brass faucet and the round table situated in the center of the kitchen imitate the aspect of old-fashioned kitchens.

Indigo is a cheerful color, appropriate for houses in the country or by the sea. It is a luminous color that aids in creating rustic ambiences.

© Pere Planells

Indigo is widely used in rustic Mediterranean kitchens, especially in hot areas close to the sea, because it is a cool and highly luminous color. In this kitchen, made of stone, indigo has been used to paint the shutters, a decorative feature typical of the Mediterranean.

© Pere Planells

Three good ideas: a wood chopping board; shelves, painted white, that serve to display some of the kitchen utensils; and a big white marble sink. This is a typical unintegrated rustic kitchen, with free-standing units placed on either side of the stove.

© Pere Planells

A practical and aesthetic solution to decorating a rustic kitchen and taking full advantage of its space is to build open shelves to store pickles, plates and everyday utensils.

© Pere Planells

© Ricardo Labougle

This rustic-style kitchen opens
directly onto the garden, where
an outdoor dining area has been
set up. In winter the home's office
serves as the main dining room
and the kitchen becomes the nerve
center of the whole house.

The structure of this kitchen is made from
polished stone, with exposed niches for
cupboards and rustic-style kitchen appliances. On the ceiling a very attractive
detail: small star-shaped skylights that
reflect light onto the kitchen floor.

© Pere Planells

© Montse Garriga

Previous page: This kitchen illustrates the essence of rustic Mediterranean style: decorative tiles that serve as a splashback, limestone-coated walls, and a white marble sink.

Above: The stone walls are an attractive aspect of the house and emphasize its authentic rustic style.

Many old kitchens disposed of chimneys that have been conserved in houses today.

© Montse Garriga

Following pages:

The cupboards of this kitchen imitate the aesthetic of the first "modern" kitchens that came out on the market. The "rural" chairs provide a cool and fresh aspect.

An old stone sink was recuperated and introduced into this kitchen, accompanied by wood furniture with knobs made of porcelain, a very appropriate material for rustic kitchens.

Integrated Kitchens

Kitchens that open into the sitting room or dining room make their presence felt; their materials and colors can be boldly integrated into the decoration of the home.

© Jan Verlinde

Opening out the kitchen into the sitting room or dining room presents a series of challenges: the layout, the choice of design for furnishings and electrical appliances, the materials, the finishing. It must be remembered that an integrated kitchen, based on the classic American model, is visible without opening any doors, and so it is important to consider every detail. When the kitchen opens into another room due to lack of space, the absence of a door permits a more rational layout of the furniture and, visually, the kitchen will seem bigger. In these cases it is advisable to use materials that are not too heavy, such as steel, aluminum and glass, as well as cold, neutral or luminous colors like gray, blue, yellow or cream. One good way to avoid overloading a space is to choose furniture with glass doors combined with lacquered finishing and unassuming handles. The secret is not to mix too many materials. In contrast, when a kitchen is integrated into a space purely for the pleasure of giving it pride of place, the best bet is to opt for natural materials, like wood, or lacquers and cladding that provide color, especially if a daring, avant-garde look is being sought.

When space is restricted, it is a good idea to use materials that are not visually dense, such as glass, either transparent or treated with acid, or stainless steel. Touches of color can be added in the details and decorative elements.

Opposite page:
Thanks to an absolutely functional use of the space, with a visually integrated kitchen, the dining and living rooms use the existing space well, making the whole floor appear larger.

© Jan Verlinde

© Jan Verlinde

© Eugeni Pons

© Eugeni Pons

© Eugeni Pons

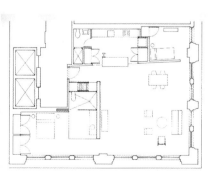

The kitchen has been separated from the dining room by a large work unit with a built-in stove and a powerful hood that stops fumes from penetrating the rest of the space.

0   1   2

The distribution of space and the absence of partitions allows for direct visibility from one end of the floor to the other– from the kitchen through to the living room.

The aluminum chairs and the metal base of the dining-room table, with casters, create a daring contrast in this space, which is dominated by the warmth of the wood, the bricks, the ochre paint and the fire glowing in the iron fireplace. This intelligent combination of materials is all that's needed to decorate a space.

© Chris Tubbs

© Chris Tubbs

The linear kitchen layout (along one wall) is the best solution in a single setting containing a sitting room, dining room, studio and kitchen.

The kitchen is not attached to a main wall and acts as a divider of various areas without the need for closed doors.

The kitchen is the first area visible on entering this house. It has been opened onto the corridor to take full advantage of the space and sunlight. The rug is an excellent idea: it marks the way into the sitting room.

© Catherine Tighe

© Catherine Tighe

© Nathan Willock

© Nathan Willock

© Nathan Willock

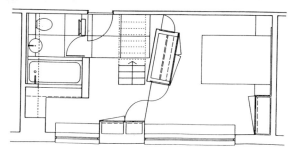

White is the most reliable color in the decoration of an integrated kitchen, especially when an effect of sobriety and luminosity is required.

Wood and glass have always been complementary: the former provides warmth and presence, the latter reduces the heaviness of wood, while its transparency improves visibility.

On the opposite page, the straight lines and pure forms of the designs define the layout.

© Eugeni Pons

© Eugeni Pons

© Eugeni Pons

© Christopher Wesnofske

© Christopher Wesnofske

© Nick Hufton (both photos)

Looking at this floor plan one can appreciate how well the space has been used. Note how a small office has been incorporated within the kitchen space.

The wooden strips stylize the design of the kitchen and provide a daring contrast to the concrete ceiling and the blue-painted element separating the studio from the dining room.

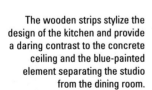

Maximum Functionality

The cooking area in this kitchen lies opposite the sink and next to the major appliances (refrigerator, oven and microwave), creating a workspace between the different work areas that makes chores easier and takes full advantage of every inch of space. The kitchen is not very large and worktops had to be installed on both sides of the cooking area, which lies in the center of a U-shape. This is extremely practical because everything required for cooking is within reach and there is no need to move from one side of the room to the other.

The fittings inside the cupboards are also designed to be as functional as possible, taking advantage of the available space and lightening the workload. Revolving shelves have been set inside the corner cupboards to make them more accessible; the drawers are divided into compartments to keep their contents in order; and stainless-steel bars have been fixed to the ledges so that the most frequently used utensils are always at hand. The office is situated next to the kitchen area, although it occupies its own independent space and benefits from abundant natural light.

© Montse Garriga (p. 56-59)

Some cabinets incorporate removable baskets that are ideal for storing fresh fruit and vegetables.

Fresh and Natural

Some of the details on display in this setting —the compact stainless-steel stove, the cart and the decoration of the dining room, which is visually integrated into the space— recall the appearance of the kitchens of years gone by. This kitchen contains the latest electrical appliances, modern furniture and a practical layout, yet its atmosphere remains reassuringly familiar.

Its coziness derives from the simplicity of the fixtures and the successful integration of the main dining room, in the style of an old country house. The wood and natural fibers, such as cane and rattan, imbue the kitchen with warmth and give the whole setting a homey feel.

© Montse Garriga (p. 60-63)

The rattan chairs give the setting a natural
touch and imbue the kitchen with warmth.

Breakfast Nook

The furniture in this kitchen has been positioned in the form of a U, to take advantage of the location of the window and of the doors leading into the garden. The experts agree that this is the most practical and complete layout possible. The two blocks on the side take full advantage of the space through the use of high cabinets, while the sink is set under the window, reveling in this wonderful source of natural light.

The most striking aspect of this kitchen is the presence of a small table— a discreet glass fixture nudging the end of the work unit. A very practical arrangement, ideal for having breakfast or a quick lunch. This kitchen emanates a relaxed atmosphere; the wood adds warmth and the pale green color on the walls provides serenity —a perfect combination for decorating a space as dynamic as a kitchen.

© Montse Garriga (p. 64-67)

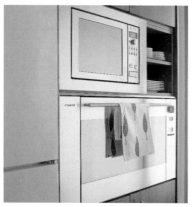

This kitchen has many innovative storage features, helping to keep it tidy and preventing anything from being mislaid.

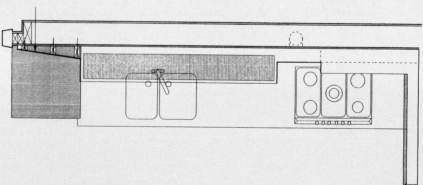

The major appliances are arranged in a line, in such a way that the sink and the cooking area are only slightly separated, which facilitates chores and reduces any unnecessary to-ing and fro-ing. Moreover, the gap between the two provides a sizeable worktop for preparing food.

The Kitchen and Children

Architect: Ash Sakula Architects
Location: London, U.K.
Photos: © Edmond Sumner

Sometimes combining kitchen chores with childcare can be a real problem. What better way to solve this than by taking advantage of the doors of the cabinets and refrigerator, appropriately clad with the same material used for school blackboards? This allows children to entertain themselves scribbling and creating their first works of art. The idea is put to work in this kitchen, where the blackboard-clad cupboards and refrigerator are an ever-changing art gallery.

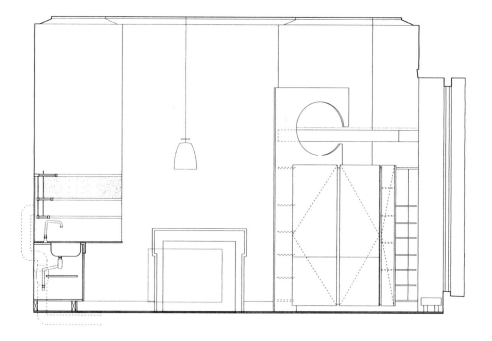

This drawing illustrates the central position of the work unit, as well as the method used to light it. Each of the kitchen areas has its own lighting, and the work unit has been treated in the same way as a dining table, with an overhead lamp with a bulb 3 feet (90 cm) from the worktop. This is the best way to light a horizontal plane without creating any shadows.

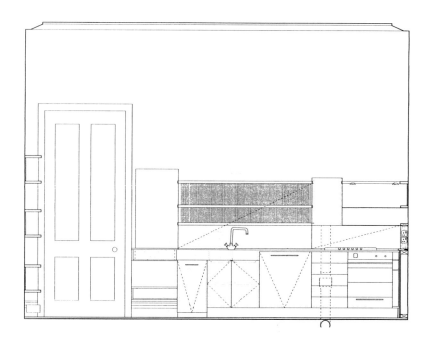

The cooking area and sink have been laid out in a block some 10 feet (3 m) long; not only is all the equipment needed for preparing food on hand, but there is plenty of elbow room too. The traditional cabinets have been substituted with a practical and decorative plate rack and several open shelves.

A kitchen island has been set in the center of the kitchen, serving both as a back-up work unit and a division between the kitchen area and the office. The pantry and the refrigerator are near the office. This layout is very practical as it eliminates the need for any long absences during family meals.

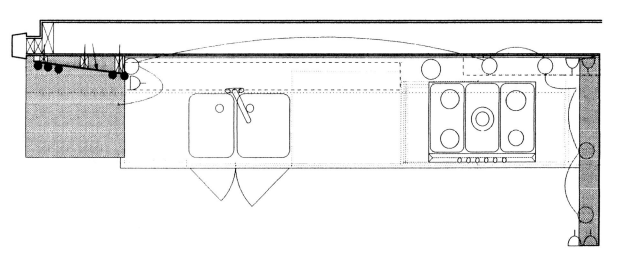

Lighting is just as important in a kitchen as the layout of the furniture. In this kitchen the worktops are impeccably lit by lamps set under the shelves, ensuring that not even the farthest corner is left in the dark. Moreover, various several have been positioned near the cooking area –ideal for using small electrical appliances without moving from the spot. Everything is within easy reach.

Everything on Show

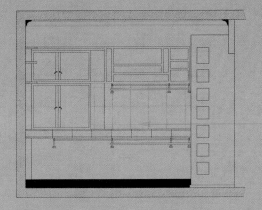

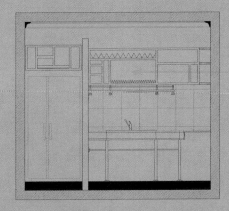

Architect: Guillermo Arias
Location: Bogotá, Colombia
Photos: © Pablo Rojas (p.74, 76, 78),
Alvaro Gutierrez (p.77)

The small electrical appliances —used almost every day in this kitchen— have been arranged in a line along the worktop. It is convenient to leave the appliances on the counter; it makes the kitchen more functional and eliminates the task of taking the applianecs out of the cabinets and putting them away again. A good cook needs his or her utensils with in easy reach. The detail in this kitchen is not only practical but also proves very attractive: the countless utensils needed to prepare exquisite dishes all hang from a steel bar.

A printed coconut-fiber mat both protects the floor and emphasizes the striking tube shape
of this kitchen, which is set at the far end of a small corridor.

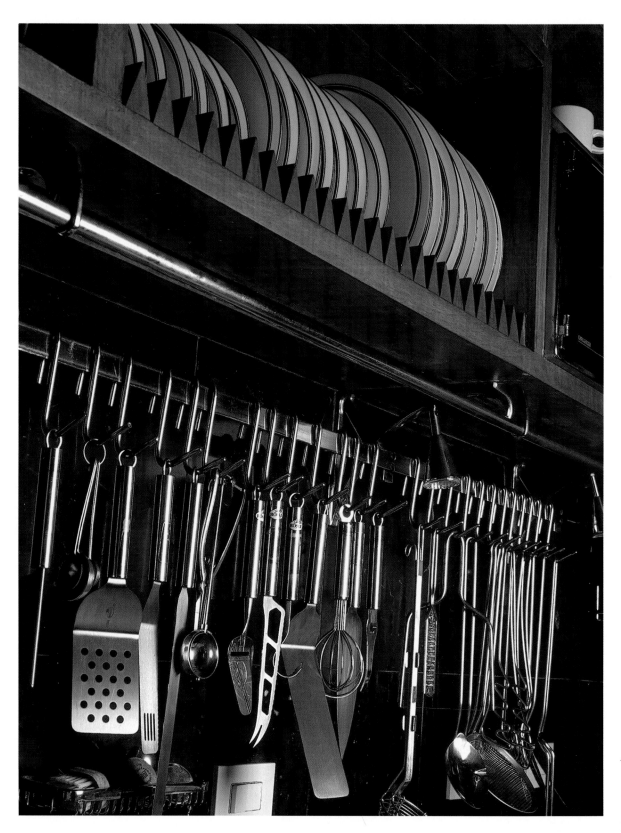

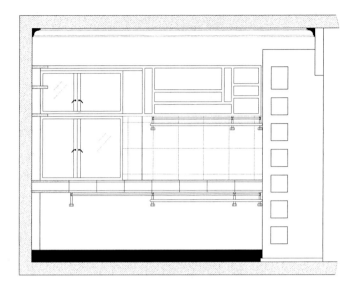

Elevation

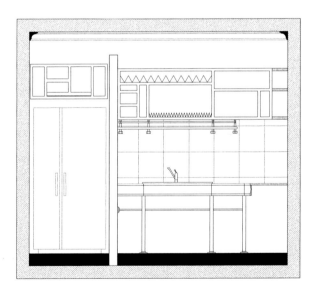

Elevation

This kitchen has no cabinets –everything is on view and within reach. The pots and pans hang from a steel bar running around the perimeter of the kitchen, underneath the work-top. Above this are shelves displaying jars of pickles and spices, a wine rack and four lamps that throw light onto the shelves.

How to Create Your Own Style

Environments
Colors and Materials

Vola by Effeti Cucine

Regula by Binova

Chatham Natural Maple by Wellborn

Spatial Conditions by Siematic (p.83)

Environments

Kitchen fixtures are constantly evolving to adapt to changing lifestyles. These days kitchen design is more flexible, spontaneous and functional. Manufacturers are creating fixtures that can be easily integrated into other household settings and in a wide variety of decorative styles.

Two well-defined trends have come to the fore: kitchens in a linear block with separate, free-standing work units that open out onto the living room or dining room; and totally deconstructed kitchens comprised of independent modules, sometimes on castors, that can be moved around as desired. This allows kitchen fixtures to be adapted to any setting or requirement.

Atlántica by Veneta Cucine

Kitchens With Sense Appeal by Poggenpohl

Sure Style Modernity by Poggenpohl

Espace by Veneta Cucine

Program 543 by Miele

Kitchen by Boffi

The influence of the professional kitchen is clearly visible in this private house.

Above left:
Línea by Leicht

Following page:
A very practical example of a kitchen with central dining table by Bulthaup.

The material defines the style: stainless steel
for modernity, handcrafted tiles for a rustic look.

Avantgarde Progam 820 by Miele

Pragma by Zanussi

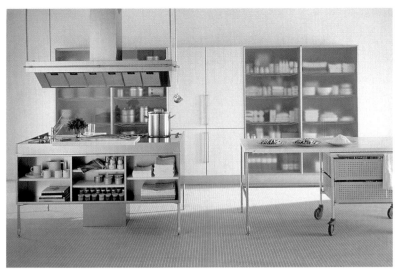

Design by Citterio for Arclinea

Opera by Binova

Louvre Clair, French Blue, Fire and Earth (below)
by Ann Sacks

High quality tiles on walls and floors are practical, resistent to heat, easy to maintain and can create very different atmospheres, as in these examples *Basque Slate* (above), *Louvre Clair* (below), *Caracol* with *Slate Floor* by Ann Sacks

Beautiful wooden kitchen furniture by Wellborn:
*Cocoa Cherry Hill Cathedral, Harbor 2 Honey
Maple* (previous page), *Prairie Med Maple*

Colors and Materials

Colors and Materials

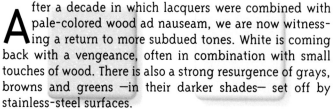

After a decade in which lacquers were combined with pale-colored wood ad nauseam, we are now witnessing a return to more subdued tones. White is coming back with a vengeance, often in combination with small touches of wood. There is also a strong resurgence of grays, browns and greens —in their darker shades— set off by stainless-steel surfaces.

The style of the present-day kitchen is moving closer and closer to that of professional installations. Stainless steel is used for appliances and worktops, in combination with wood, lacquers and laminated finishing. Glass treated with acid is also popular, as it is easy to maintain and adds light to a space; it can even be used to protect walls, in place of traditional tiles.

The fact that the kitchen has regained its leading role in the home and now opens out more onto other spaces has made it necessary to use lighter and more visually attractive materials.

Previous pages: *The Colors of the Corian* by Corian

The following examples are courtesy of Axiom

The color scheme:
There is a growing trend towards the use of bolder and brighter colors in the home. Taking its influences from around the world along with heritage tones, COLOR helps create individuality and expression.

Creating the look:
Consider using all the surfaces within the kitchen to build a layered and coordinated look, starting with your chosen palette of colors. With an increasing choice of available colors in all kitchen products, an exciting look can now be achieved to suit each individual style.

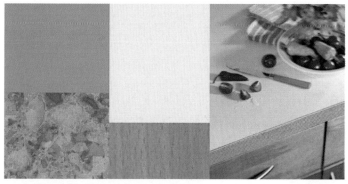

Fresh yellow and warm timber with a green accent.

Colored natural textures with a blue highlight.

The new neutral Scheme:
NEW NEUTRAL takes the cool grey palette and adds a touch of warmth to create a softer environment within the home. This contemporary look uses the latest materials and finishes and combines clean lines and high technology.

Creating the look:
Warm greys and soft textures are combined with accent colors to create an extensive palette around a simple mood. NEW NEUTRAL is the perfect setting for the professional/industrial appliances found in today's modern kitchens.

Cool greys with a tint of light pear or maple.

Soft silvers complementing natural stone textures.

The rustic style:
RUSTIC uses autumnal, earthy and natural tones to create richness and warmth within the home. The use of natural colors and materials provides the ideal backdrop for old and new furniture.

Creating the look:
RUSTIC uses warm and hot colors in combination with rich woods such as cherry and oak. Naturally pigmented paints can enhance the appearence of an "aged" look within the kitchen. Additional coarse-textured materials such as terra-cotta, woven baskets and stone help to build an authentic RUSTIC look.

Natural textures combined with rich cherry wood.

Strongly textured worktops with blue granite and cream.

The contrast style:
The CONTRAST style is all about opposites. This highly contemporary and distinctive look uses light and dark finishes in a striking way to create drama and impact within the home. CONTRAST is a sophisticated look often described in style magazines as east meets west.

Creating the look:
CONTRAST uses cream and white colors in conjunction with strong woods such as teak, rosewood and wenge. Surfaces may be a combination of shiny and matte together with small areas of strong accent color.

White, cream, and light woods contrasting with rich dark timbers.

Shiny black granite and metallics contrasting with warm pear or maple.

Kitchens:
Bits and Pieces

Fixtures
Tables
Electrical Appliances
Details
The Kitchen of the Future

All models by Siematic

BISCUIT   FARINE   PÂT

Fixtures

Fixtures

The designers of kitchen fixtures have made a special effort to solve the problem of storage for the utensils and foodstuffs needed in a kitchen. Their solutions range from storage towers that occupy only eight inches of floor space —perfect for small kitchens— to practical cabinets with an interior configuration that makes it easy to fill them up in an orderly fashion.

Below left: Furniture detail by Poggenpohl
Center: *Regula* by Binova
Right: Sink module with storage space by Miele
Following page: Adjustable cupboards by Siematic

Effective storage systems for every need
by Siematic

Previous page: Sink with extractable wooden shelves.

Cabinets by Poggenpohl in various heights with clever interior distributions offer space for any household goods.

Specialized storage units by Siematic

Custom-made drawers by Siematic keep everything handy.

Italian design by Binova

Following page:
Furniture details by Poggenpohl

Prizewinning design by Siematic

Accessories for drawers and pull outs.

Alu 2000 by Poggenpohl (above and below right)

Country by Binova

Drawer by Siematic

Poggenpohl: Fronts FK 958 in chestnut and
blue satin-frosted glass

Life by Miele, a retrospective design

Following pages:
Program 554 by Miele, in brown-red cherry

Romantic by Miele

Tables

Tables

The table is an essential feature of a modern kitchen, and it is easy to find tables in a wide range of shapes and sizes that can be adapted to any space.

The predominant material is wood, because it adds warmth to the setting, or glass combined with steel legs, which provide a light touch that is perfect for small kitchens with an avant-garde feel.

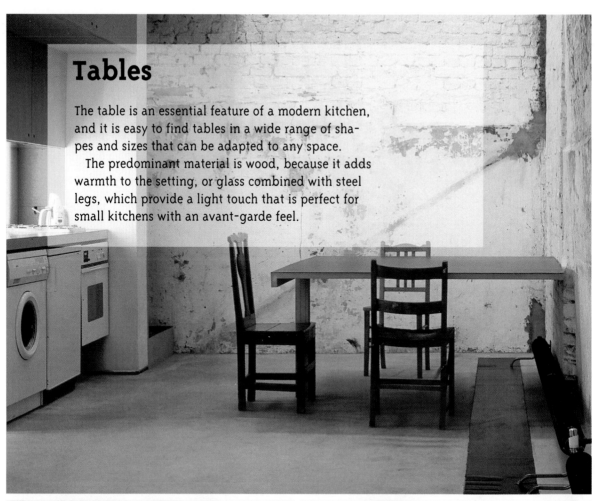

Kitchen bar *Prairie Light Maple* by Wellborn

P. 130:
The freedom of planning with Siematic-Modula

Free-standing kitchen modules by Bulthaup

Carts by Alessi

The elegant design of Citterio combines well with a rustic table and stools.

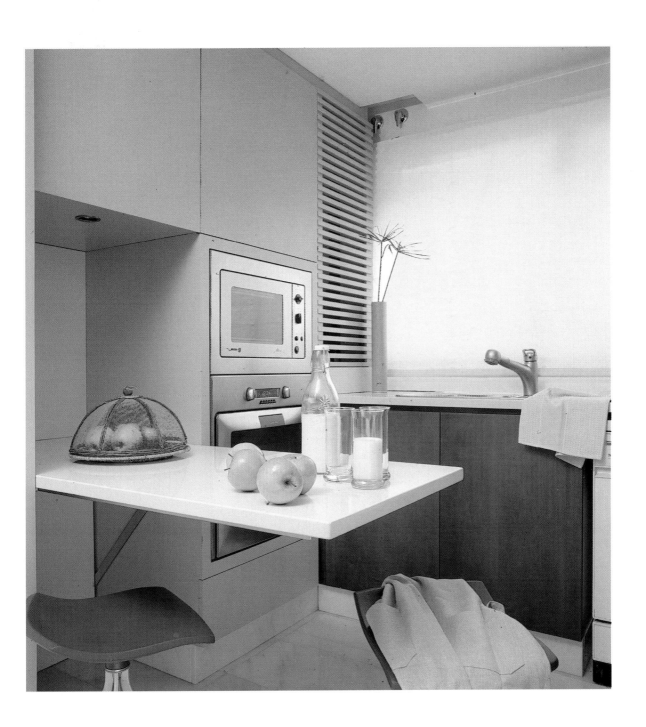

A homage to the kitchens of our ancestors
by Chalon

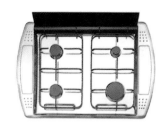

Electrical Appliances

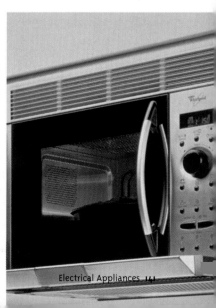

Electrical appliances

Cabinets and drawers for storing food are becoming bigger and more accessible, while the design of electrical appliances has improved so much that they sometimes find themselves the undisputed stars of a kitchen.

Top: *Brio Brio* by Aiko

Ceramic stovetops by Franke

Left: *Artusi*, the philosophy of free-standing, by Arclinea

Following page:
Gas stoves by Franke (top and bottom)

Brio Brio by Aiko (center)

Stoves

Ovens incorporated in the wall by Whirlpool, AKG 637/IX (above right) *FI 1029 IN* by Rosières (right) and Gaggenau (left)

A wall of cabinets in dark walnut incorporates the oven, refrigerator, dishwasher and a roomy pantry unit: *Weiss Weiss* by Aiko

Ovens

Eco Tech Ind. by Franke

Legend Granite Ind. by Franke

Miele Classic

Turbo Ronda Ind. by Franke

Miele

Super-Tech by Franke

Maxi Tech Ind. by Franke with multifunction and easy-cleaning system

Pyroli-Tech by Franke

Maxi 90 Ind. by Franke

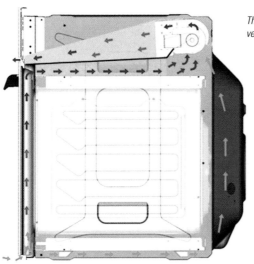

The airflow of the ventilation system

Concealable vent by Gaggenau

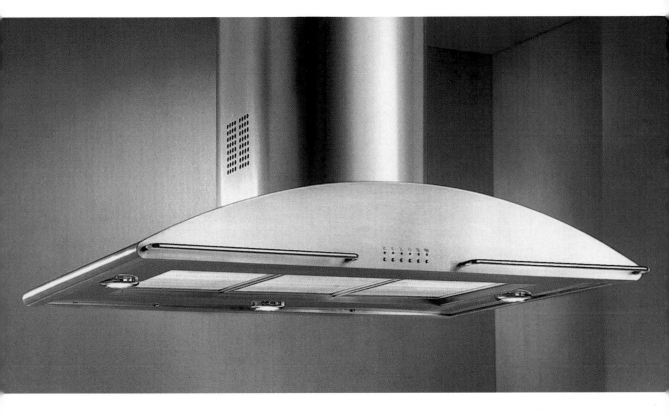

Vents

Model by Candy

Model for a freestanding stove by Gaggenau

Model by Rosières

Model by Candy

Microwave above vent M.A.C. by Whirlpool

Microwaves

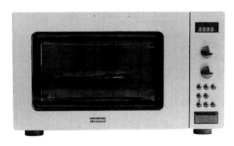

FR-700CB by Daewoo (top and left)

Side by Side by Gaggenau

Refrigerator and freezer fitted underneath worktop by Candy

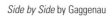

Old Style by Rosières

Refrigerators

These refrigerators by Whirlpool change their color at night

Details

Details

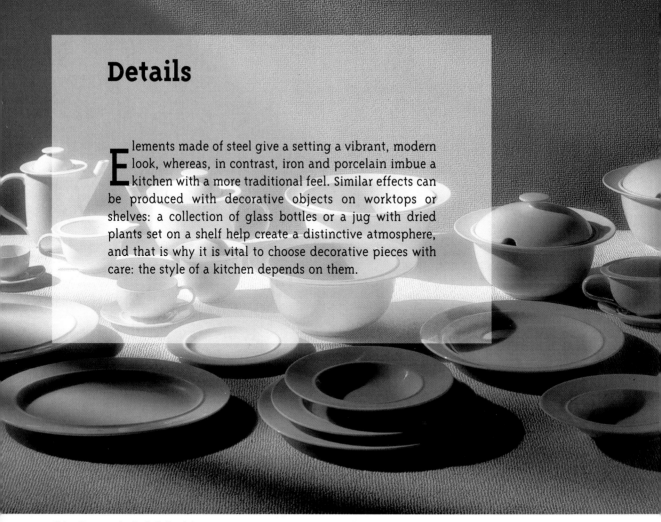

Elements made of steel give a setting a vibrant, modern look, whereas, in contrast, iron and porcelain imbue a kitchen with a more traditional feel. Similar effects can be produced with decorative objects on worktops or shelves: a collection of glass bottles or a jug with dried plants set on a shelf help create a distinctive atmosphere, and that is why it is vital to choose decorative pieces with care: the style of a kitchen depends on them.

China dinner service *La Bella Tavola* by Alessi (top and bottom right)

Kettel by Alessi

Colorful accessories by Electrolux

Corkscrew *Anna G.* by Alessi

Espresso machines by Alessi: *Nespresso*

La Cupola, designed by Aldo Rossi,
in aluminium and black

Stackable multiuse modules to delight the most modern culinary techniques

The Kitchen of the Future

All photos in these pages courtesy of Electrolux

Prototype Screenfridge, the new center for domestic communication

The technological capabilities of the newest electrical appliances seem to belong to the future: among the countless innovations on the market, we can find refrigerators computerized that notify consumers when an item is out of stock and ovens that automatically control their cooking times. New technologies have arrived, making our daily chores easier.

Udu, a new concept to store delivered, internet bought groceries

Live-in by Zanussi connects all electrical appliances and organizes the domestic work

More than a table: on this new element you can prepare food, cook and store culinary objects inside.

Celebrating cooking as an art with *Podium*

Munch, a fun way to cover your plates

EME-0980 is a small microwave with a new design: easy to use, easy to transport

Integration incorporates a microwave in a conventional stove; an ideal solution for small spaces.

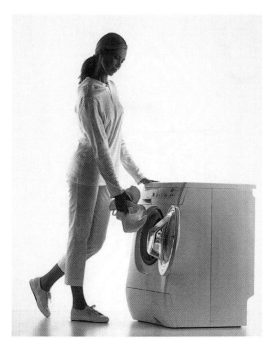

12 by Zanussi measures the quantity and degree of dirtiness before starting the washing process.

Podium, the last generation of stoves features
interactive heating systems for pans with
temperature sensor.

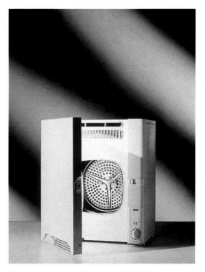

The dimensions of the dryer *TCS-172E* are reduced to a minimum without losing power.

IQ prepares several plates at the same time. It can be used in any part of the house due to its friendly design.

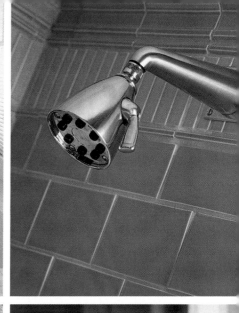

Baths

A Whole World to Enjoy

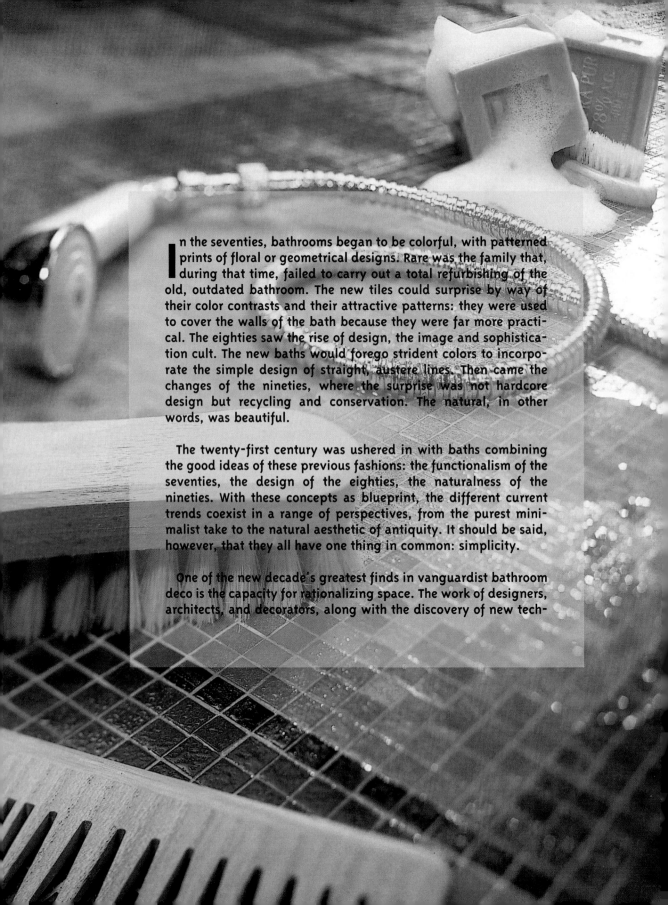

In the seventies, bathrooms began to be colorful, with patterned prints of floral or geometrical designs. Rare was the family that, during that time, failed to carry out a total refurbishing of the old, outdated bathroom. The new tiles could surprise by way of their color contrasts and their attractive patterns: they were used to cover the walls of the bath because they were far more practical. The eighties saw the rise of design, the image and sophistication cult. The new baths would forego strident colors to incorporate the simple design of straight, austere lines. Then came the changes of the nineties, where the surprise was not hardcore design but recycling and conservation. The natural, in other words, was beautiful.

The twenty-first century was ushered in with baths combining the good ideas of these previous fashions: the functionalism of the seventies, the design of the eighties, the naturalness of the nineties. With these concepts as blueprint, the different current trends coexist in a range of perspectives, from the purest minimalist take to the natural aesthetic of antiquity. It should be said, however, that they all have one thing in common: simplicity.

One of the new decade's greatest finds in vanguardist bathroom deco is the capacity for rationalizing space. The work of designers, architects, and decorators, along with the discovery of new tech-

niques and materials, has made it possible to solve problems in decoration which, a mere few years ago, were not even receiving mention. An example: today the bath's lighting is more essential than its having a large tub. And visual openness is more desirable than filling the room with ornaments. Designs are purer, simpler. The idea is not to have them overlooked, but to call attention to them. Just look at the forms of today's water-saving toilet tanks, faucets, or tubs.

Materials are a critical component of any decorative style, and in the bathroom they take on special relevance because of the need to deal with humidity, heavy contact with water, and use. Just as ceramics dominated the seventies, marble the eighties, and wood the nineties, today's choice would be new paints, natural stone, glass, and steel. An "ideal" material is nonexistent, but in the majority of cases a designer opts to takes into account aesthetics and functionalism, balancing both while eventually having to favor one or the other. The vanguardist bathroom experiments with materials once shunned by decorators, such as cement or aluminum. Paint now comes into almost every setting: sometimes to bring out wall textures/materials through color, sometimes to cause a striking sensation of negative space, of order. What is in these days is the aseptic, purist, but well-planned bathroom.

Different Styles

Modern Bathrooms
Minimalist Bathrooms
Rustic Bathrooms
Integrated Bathrooms

Modern Bathrooms

The modern bathroom is both daring and innovative. It proves that functionality and beauty are not mutually exclusive.

© Chris Gascoigne (VIEW)

© Stephen Varady and Rusell Pell

The synthetic washbasin is slightly transparent and creates a visual interplay with the vertical mirror. The wall has been painted with lacquer to give it a sheen.

© Matteo Piazza

When space is limited it is a good idea to use transparent glass partitions and halogen lamps.

The washbasin has been placed on a thin sheet of glass supported by two wooden legs. The whole room is reflected in the mirror that covers one entire wall.

© Matteo Piazza

A modern bathroom is perhaps the most complicated type of bathroom to decorate. An avant-garde bathroom not only strives for beauty and visual flair, it also seeks to combine these two concepts with functional considerations. Some good opportunities can be found in a modern bathroom: experiments with new materials, mixtures of very different materials and a practical approach to spatial arrangements. We could say that functionality and the exploitation of space and natural light are, along with innovative design, the essential characteristics of a modern bathroom. Materials such as glass and wood are fundamental: the former provides airy, luminous settings, while the latter offers warmth, comfort and functionality.

Another consideration in an avant-garde bathroom is the layout: each function has a specific area and, where there is enough space, these areas are marked off by partitions (almost always made of glass) or other elements that visually separate the different functions.

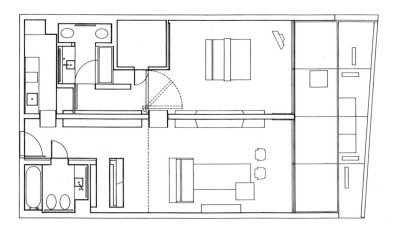

© Markus Tomaselli Rataplan

A large partition made of vertical glass strips separates the bathroom from the rest of the house. The most intimate area is hidden behind the blue screen.

© Markus Tomaselli Rataplan

The exploitation of natural light is one of the main aims of modern architecture. This bathroom provides a good example, with compartments made of transparent glass that allow the sunlight to penetrate the entire space.

© Duccio Malagamba

The base of the washbasin has also been used to enclose the bathtub, thus creating a compact structure. A large closet, which also serves as a dressing room, has been built in opposite the bathroom area.

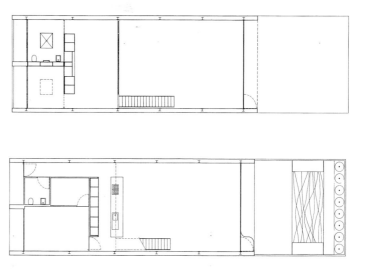

Minimalist Bathrooms

The main characteristic of the mini-malist bathroom is the absence of any bright colors and decorative details that might distract from the purity of the forms.

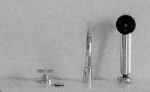

© Alberto Piovano

The minimalist style can be cold and austere in a bathroom, due to the absence of any striking colors or sensuous shapes. The basis of a minimalist bathroom is the use of one or, at most, two materials, along with neutral colors, such as white, gray and various textures of stone. This restraint is the only way to maintain the simplicity of form that is so essential to this style. Even the faucets are usually set into the wall and their design is as simple as possible.

One of the advantages of minimalism is that it conveys a great sense of order. It is therefore a good idea to exploit the characteristics of this style in bathrooms where space or natural light are restricted. It is also a perfect way to stress the architectural features of a space, as in the bathroom shown on this page. The absence of any bright colors or decorative details throws the spotlight onto the structure of the room, the thickness of the walls and the shape of the elements.

© Alberto Piovano

Sunlight pours into this space, becoming an integral part of the concept for this bathroom, which is dominated by whitened concrete.

© Alberto Piovano

The bathtub is completely square, as is the surrounding space. The plan illustrates its central position, a detail that reinforces the minimalist decoration.

This bathroom is an example of minimalism at its most extreme. A single material has been used for the decoration, thereby boldly showing off the purity of the design and the forms.

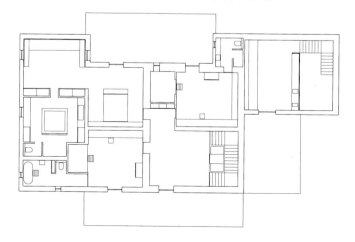

The sink and stone top comprise a single unit. A slight slope in the faucet area prevents water from spilling.

In this case, the sink is a marble tub with the faucet handle set in one side.

The bathtub has been built with the same material as the sink to emphasize the bathroom's geometric lines.

© Margheritta Spiluttini

The bathtub takes pride of place and
benefits from the sunshine pouring
through the skylight.

The L-shaped position of
the bathrooms makes the most
of the space and promotes
mobility between areas.

In order to take full advantage of the
space, the bidet and toilet have been
fitted into a wall clad with wood.

© Hélène Binet

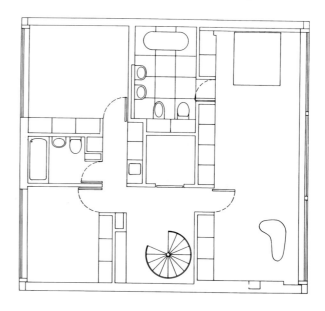

© Jordi Miralles

A large rectangular mirror runs along the entire length of the wall, reflecting light on a bathroom that revolves around the contrast between black and white. The design of both the bathtub and the washbasins is extremely stark.

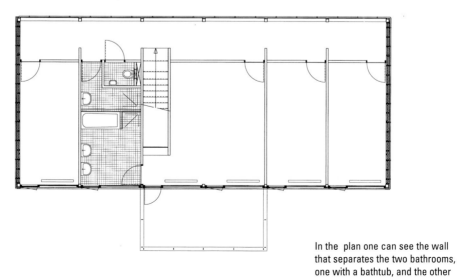

In the plan one can see the wall that separates the two bathrooms, one with a bathtub, and the other with a shower.

© Reiner Lautwein

© Reiner Lautwein

This bathroom illustrates how minimalism can be an inspired solution for bathrooms in a confined space. The glass, granite and white tiles all add lightness to the setting.

The bathroom contains a very compact surface area. The elements have been cleverly positioned, drawing attention to the washbasin on one of the lateral walls.

Interior design by:
Claire Bataille & Paul Ibens

The floor and the bathtub are both made from granite. This results in a unified simplicity.

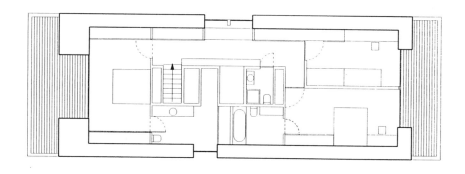

An opaque glass panel, open at both sides, isolates the shower from the washbasin area and so serves as an elegant and practical partition.

This spacious bathroom incorporates a large frosted-glass structure to separate the washbasin area from the more intimate space. The bases of the two sinks, set side by side, are totally cylindrical and made of dark wood.

Rustic Bathrooms

The rustic-style bathroom is inspired by the bathrooms in old country houses. Its elements are made of painted cement, natural stone or wood.

© Pere Planells

© Pere Planells

Tiles combined with paint, or earthenware tiles matched with pebble stones are just some of the materials used to decorate rustic or Mediterranean-style bathrooms, as can be seen from the bathroom on this page. The floor is usually covered with earthenware tiles —sometimes placed loosely, unconnected by cement, or embellished with wooden inlays and decorative friezes— although we can also find wood (especially in urban settings) and concrete, either painted or in its natural color. The pebbled floors, like the one in this bathroom, are usually original, although these days a technique called imprinted cement is used to achieve an almost perfect imitation of this traditional design. The walls are clad to half their height (from 1.50 to 1.80 meters/5 to 6 feet) with handmade tiles, to protect the areas that come in contact with water. The rest of the wall is painted in a plain color, although sometimes special techniques are used to imitate the uneven surfaces found on the walls of old houses.

Rustic sinks are similar to those in rustic kitchens, with stone or concrete supports and tops made of natural materials.

© Pere Planells

The generous proportions of this bathroom have made it possible to create different areas: the sink and the big bathtub opposite it and, to the rear, the shower with its unclad walls. The platform with wooden planking is a good idea: it provides access to the bathtub and, at the same time, it divides the space in half.

Two bathrooms featuring several of the colors that dominate the rustic style. The one on the left combines white tiles with ochre paint, while the one on the right boldly displays a mixture of green, indigo and ochre.

© Pere Planells

© Pere Planells

The walls around the bathtub have been clad with glossy tiles to protect them against humidity. The rest of the wall has been painted a stunning pistachio green, giving the bathroom a dash of brio.

The charm of this bathroom derives from the concrete wall, which has been given a coat of green paint. The concrete is textured and not completely smooth, giving the setting a rustic touch. The washbasin and the table present a great visual simplicity.

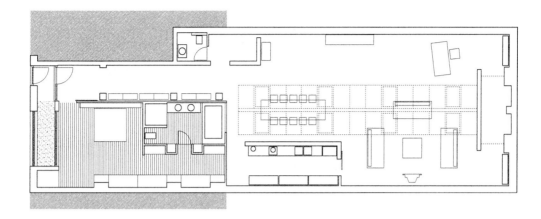

© Maite Gallardo

The bathtub has been situated on one side of the space and the shower adjacent to the toilet opposite. An open door reveals a pair of built-in washbasins.

The large size of the bathroom has made it possible to create compartments using partitions. This provides greater convenience as several people can use the bathroom at the same time without any loss of privacy. The decorative style is not only determined by the materials (concrete on the walls and wood on the floor) but also by the vibrant combination of colors.

The concrete inside the shower has been clad with the same tiles as the bathtub. Only the upper part of the wall has been painted, again in green, setting it off against the bright blue of the ceiling. To the left of the shower, a toilet built into the wall, with its cistern fitted into the lower wall, adds a modern touch to this rustic style.

Rustic Bathrooms **197**

© Pere Planells

A structure made with
building blocks provides the
base for a wooden countertop,
which has been treated
to withstand contact with
water. Designed to hold
towels and other bathroom
items, and its form follows the
contours of the stone wall.

This bathroom retains the original color of the old wooden beams, emphasizing the rustic style of the decoration. The shower is marked off by a slight slope in the earthenware floor and, as its surrounding base is very large, is not defined any further. The bathroom has a door that leads directly onto the garden.

© Pere Planells

© Pere Planells

Integrated Bathrooms

Bathrooms that are integrated into other spaces acquire an unaccustomed prominence and endow a setting with great character.

© Eugeni Pons

Integrating a bathroom into another space —normally the master bedroom requires a large area with plenty of light. The possibilities are more limited in a confined space, and in these cases it may be better to integrate only the washbasin or bathtub and put the other elements in a separate room. An old bathtub (or a new design, in an avant-garde setting) placed in the bedroom area, without any separation, works well if a strong visual impact is sought. This solution gives a space great character. Integrating the washbasin, as in the bathroom on the opposite page, can prove very practical, as it allows several people to use the bathroom facilities at the same time without disturbing each other.

In many homes it is possible to knock down dividing walls to create bigger, loftlike spaces. This not only results in a few extra feet but also allows more sunlight to enter. This option must first be discussed with an architect, as only an expert can offer solutions for substituting the master walls of a house with some kind of pillars that ensure the stability of the architectural structure.

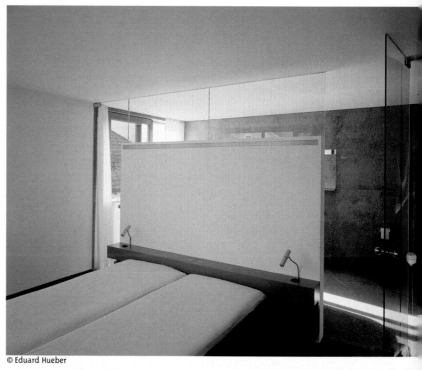

© Eduard Hueber

The bathroom and bedroom share the space, although each occupies a clearly defined area. A partition separates the two without completely shutting off the space; there are no doors but access is available from either side. The upper part of the screen is made of glass, to allow more light to enter the bedroom.

© Eduard Hueber

On the opposite page, a concrete block provides the base for a fitted steel sink. The contrast between the materials adds character to the space.

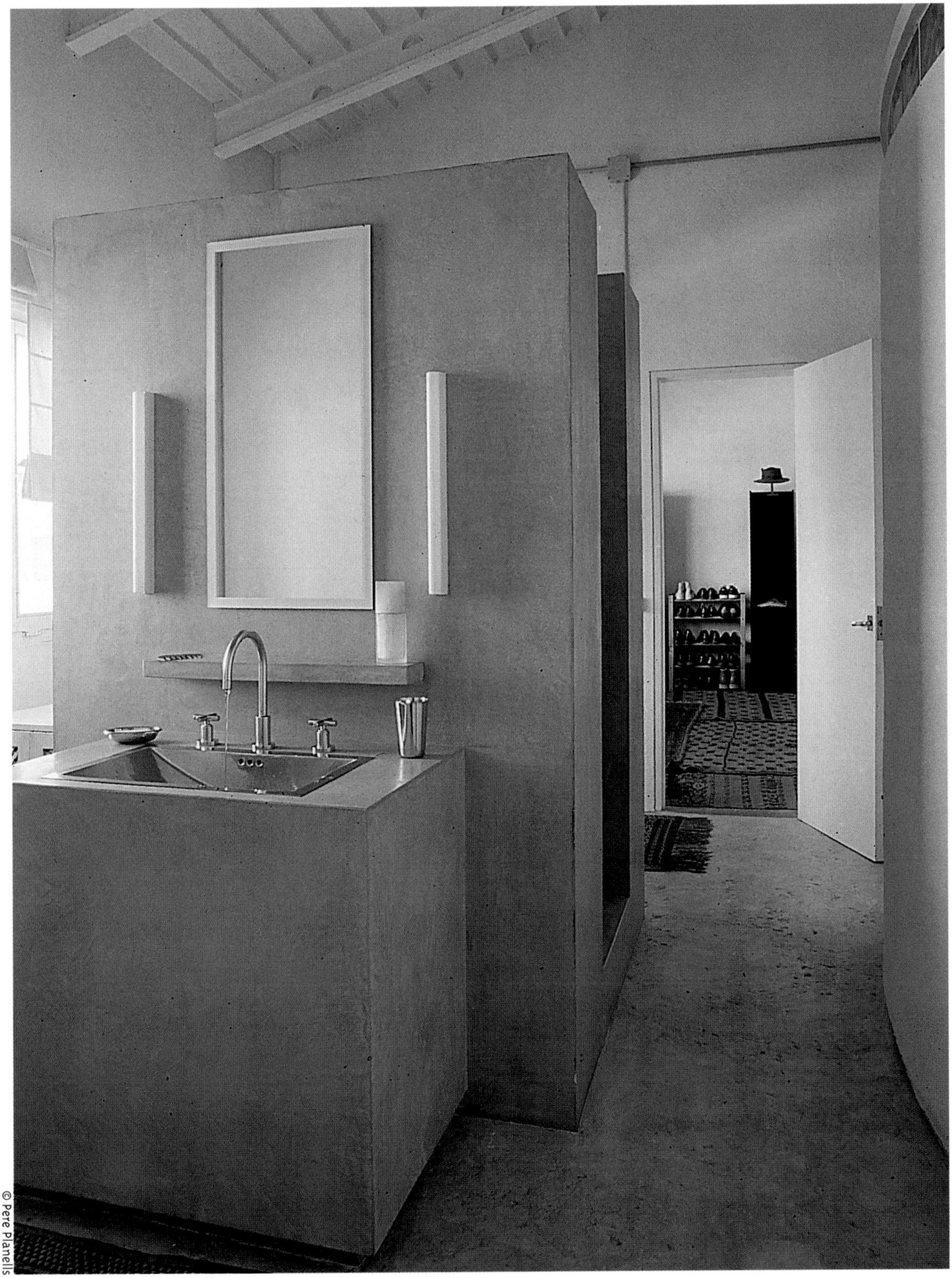

© Pere Planells

Straight lines and a striking trough-like sink are the key elements of this space. In order to combine serenity with a strong visual impact, both the sink and counter are made of wood, which has been specially treated to withstand humidity. All the walls are white, except the one at the rear, which is clad with tile.

© Peter Aaron (Esto)

In this house the washbasin has been installed half-way down the corridor leading to the sitting room to take advantage of spare space in the building's structure.

The wall of the corridor curves out slightly, providing space for the shower and toilet.

The glass wall gives the shower some wonderful views of the garden. The washbasin is a stone cube.

© Shinkenshiku-sha

© Peter Aaron (Esto)

The plan illustrates the curved wall, a solution which gains space in the bathroom and prevents the hallway from becoming a tube.

© Chris Tubbs

The bathroom occupies the main space in this loft and it is daringly exposed to view.

All the elements of the bathroom have been placed on top of a platform; this is the only feature that marks off the area.

The location of the bathroom and its prominence are reflected in the floor plan. One can also see how the kitchen opens out into the large empty space.

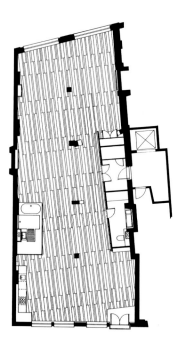

© Chris Tubbs

© Andreas Wagner

Sliding doors can be moved along tracks to either conceal or reveal the bathroom, as desired. The photo on the right illustrates another good idea for making the most of space: the washbasin has been set on top of one of the ends of the bathtub, while the mirror reflects the setting, creating the illusion of greater depth.

© Andreas Wagner

Marble Bathroom

Architect: Guillermo Arias
Location: Bogotá, Colombia
Photos: © Pablo Rojas (p. 210),
  Alvaro Gutierrez (p. 212 a 215)

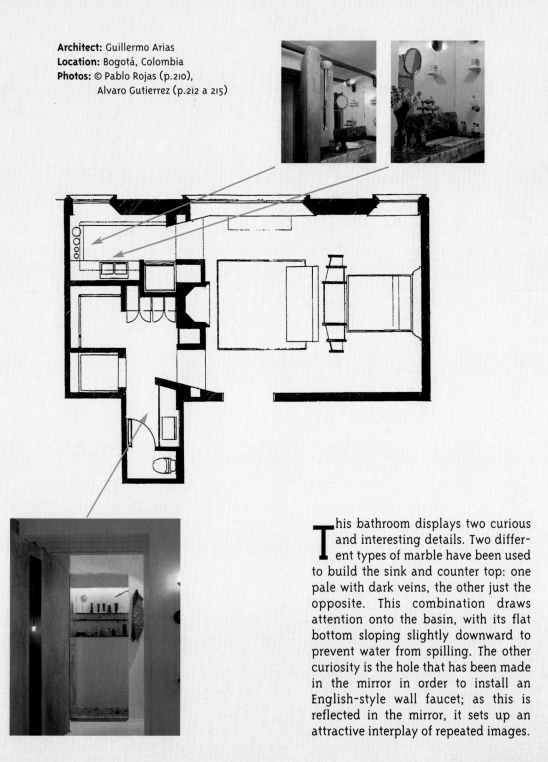

This bathroom displays two curious and interesting details. Two different types of marble have been used to build the sink and counter top: one pale with dark veins, the other just the opposite. This combination draws attention onto the basin, with its flat bottom sloping slightly downward to prevent water from spilling. The other curiosity is the hole that has been made in the mirror in order to install an English-style wall faucet; as this is reflected in the mirror, it sets up an attractive interplay of repeated images.

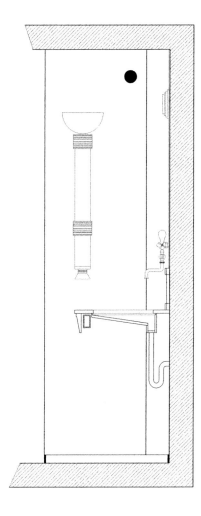

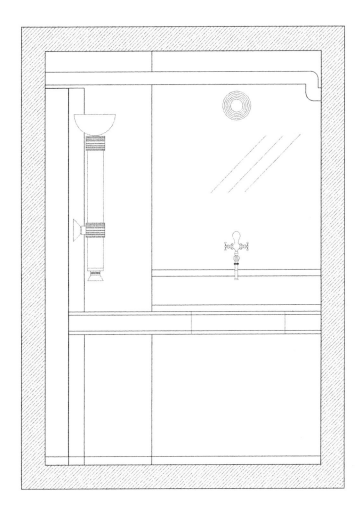

Sink section

Sink elevation

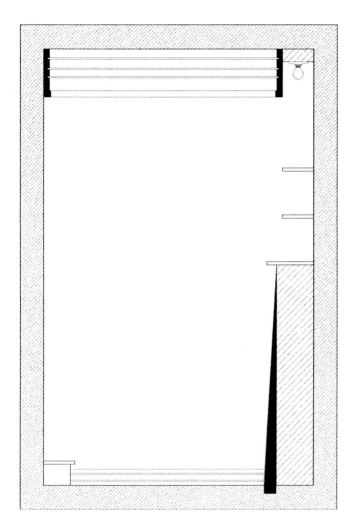

Shower section

Shower elevation

How to Create Your Own Style

Environments
Colors
Materials

Environments

Environments

The concept of the bathroom environment has also evolved. Little by little the pleasure of enjoying a few moments of relaxation in a big bathtub is being rediscovered. Showers do not substitute tubs; the two complement each other, with one helping to alleviate the early-morning rush and the providing an opportunity to wind down after a long working day.

Hydromassage tubs, thermostatic showers and even saunas all now have their place in the modern bathroom. In any style of bathroom, the environment can be adapted and modified through the use of different furniture pieces ane decorative elements. Alternatives to cabinets under the sink or open shelves include carts, cabinets in the form of a tower that take sup minimal floor space, or even wooden chests and cane baskets.

Shower *Pluvia* designed by
Matteo Thun for Rapsel, sink
Ninfo designed by Ramón
Ubeda for Rapsel, accessories
Cinizia's Familiy by Nito.

The clean-lined design by well-known designers
as Norman Foster (previous page above) and
Philippe Starck for Duravit's bathroom
fittings creates modern urban environments.

Tate and *Kuo Lavatories* by Ann Sacks

Serie 1930 by Duravit

Colors

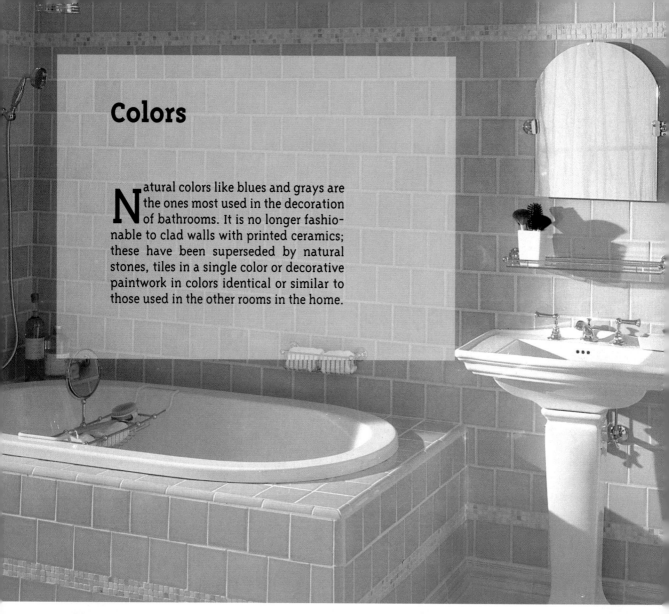

Colors

Natural colors like blues and grays are the ones most used in the decoration of bathrooms. It is no longer fashionable to clad walls with printed ceramics; these have been superseded by natural stones, tiles in a single color or decorative paintwork in colors identical or similar to those used in the other rooms in the home.

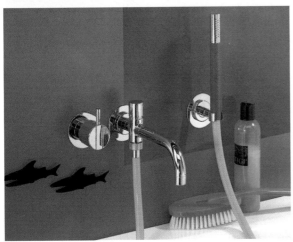

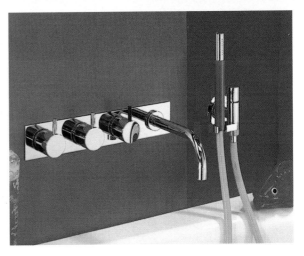

Materials

Materials

Besides porcelain and ceramics, other materials have gained prominence in bathroom design: treated wood, steel, glass and synthetic moldings, and concrete structures as the basic elements for delineating space. Just as kitchens have adapted to the decoration of sitting rooms, so bathrooms have adapted to bedrooms by taking advantage of forms and materials that were once reserved for more exalted settings.

Piel Leather by Ann Sacks (below left), *Euclide* (center) and *Nost* (right) by Rapsel

Following page: *Kuo Oval Lavatory* by Ann Sacks

Mongolfiere, colorful tiles, by Bardelli

Soli e Lune by Bardelli

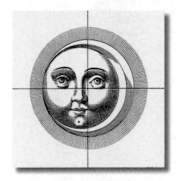

Bathrooms:
Bits and Pieces

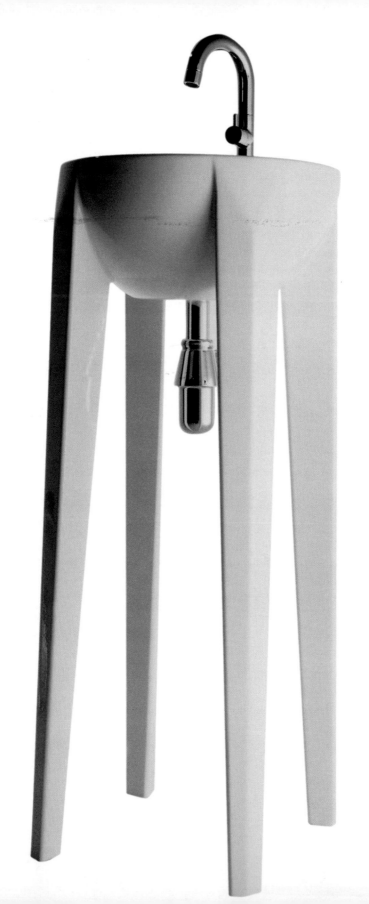

Sinks

Sinks

A wide array of sink styles made of different materials are available for every design —from rustic to minimal to English-style. Every setting has a washbasin that is ideally suited to it.

Previous pages:
Ninfo Collection by Rapsel

AQ2 by ArtQuitect Edition (above),
Philippe Starck design for Duravit
(sink) and Hansgrohe (faucet)
(below left), *Happy D.* by Duravit
(center and right)

Titanio by Flaminia

Bol by Roca

Fontana by Roca

Following page:
Serie 1930 by Duravit

Vero by Duravit

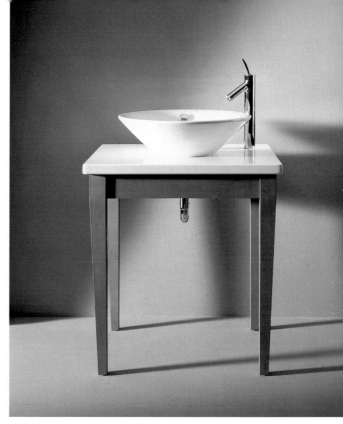

Qbk by Altro

Philippe Starck Edition 1 by Duravit

Vero by Duravit

Philippe Starck Edition 1 by Duravit

Ecoloomvi by Altro with mirror in the same translucent color.

Positano by Rapsel

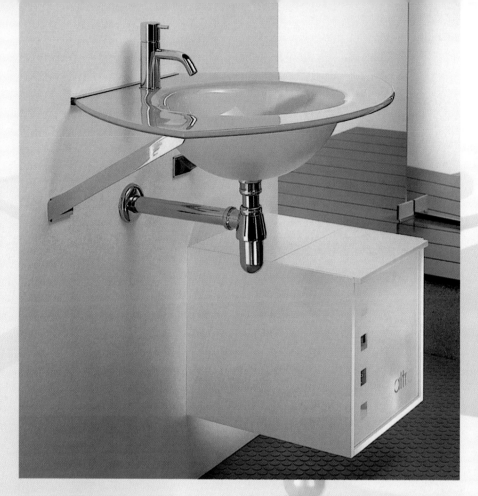

Sink *Ecoloom* and cabinet *Elements* by Altro

Play of light: A stainless steel sink fixed to a wall of mosaic tiles – *Le Gemme 20* by Bisazza

Princess Yellow by Ann Sacks

Tate Deck by Ann Sacks

Reservoir by Ann Sacks

Reservoir in green by Ann Sacks

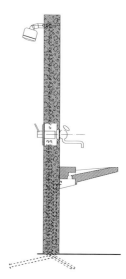

An old Turkish toilet found on the site and cleaned with acid was transformed into an original sink of a Portuguese country house. A shower is installed on the other side of the partition wall, which uses the same water installations.

AQ1 by ArtQuitect
AQ7 by ArtQuitect

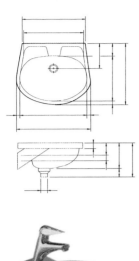

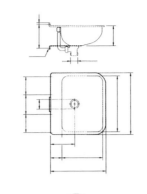

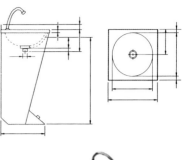

BR-280 by Franke

Nasi by Franke

LP-21 by Franke

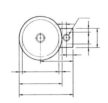

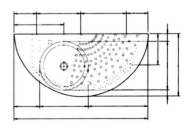

LMX-38 by Franke

BS-205 by Franke

CRL-5 by Franke

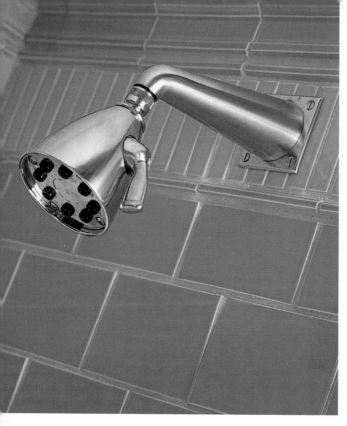

Birmingham showerhead by Ann Sacks

Odisea by Ramón Soler

Odisea by Ramón Soler

Benson by Ann Sacks

Faucets

Faucets

The single-control faucet system has proved so functional that fewer dual-control models are being manufactured. In visual terms, the single control is better suited to bathrooms with a minimalist or avant-garde design, while faucets with dual controls are still the best option for rustic or English-style settings.

Tate wall mounted (left), *One* (center), *Tate* (right) by Ann Sacks

Following page:
Reservoir (above, below right) and *Benson* (below left) by Ann Sacks

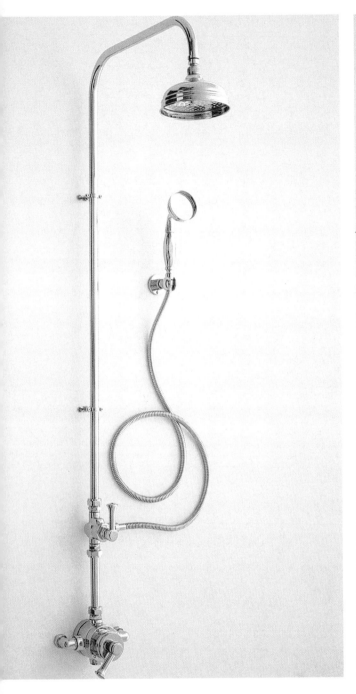

Benson, thermostatic exposed shower,
by Ann Sacks

Reservoir, concealed shower, by Ann Sacks

Benson, monobloc bidet,
by Ann Sacks

Birmingham, monobloc bidet,
by Ann Sacks

Showers

Showers

Showers can be custom made or prefabricated, and both options offer a wide range of possibilities with respect to their design and materials. In a large bathroom one solution is that a shower cabin incorporates thermostatic faucets and a sauna effect.

A different look: Elegant design by
Arne Jacobson for Vola

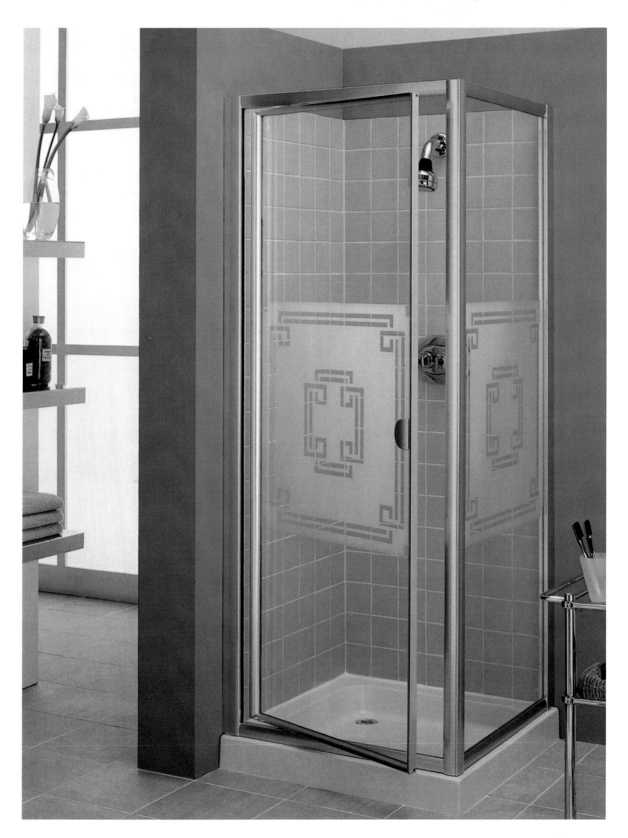

QUARTZ by Roca

QUARTZ 2MR by Roca

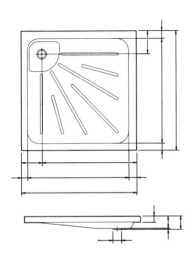

BS-400 by Franke

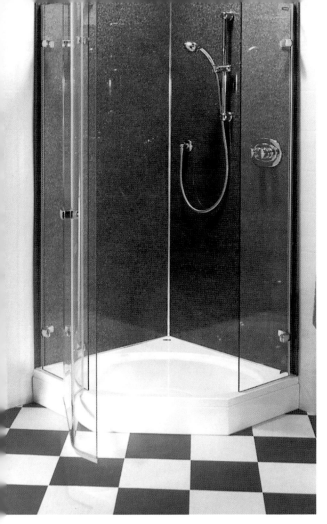

Shower panel *7500 Noir Envision* by Formica

Trevi Modern Pivot by Trevi

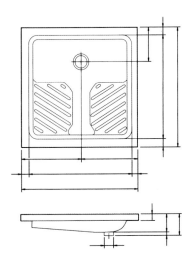

BS-500 by Franke

Filjet by Albatros delivers three fine
jets of water

XTOOL, Intelligence by Dornbracht

Djerba by Jacob Delafon

Kattara by Jacob Delafon

Punch by Jacob Delafon

New Haven by Villeroy & Bosch

Trocadero by Jacob Delafon

Báltica by Jacob Delafon

Sweetjet by Albatros emits nebulized jets of water

Rolljet by Albatros releases a small spiralling swirl that massages the body

Pluvia 130 Bianco by Albatros

Bathtubs

Bathtubs

The pleasure of a hot bath can be had in an array of bathtubs that set different moods depending on their form and style. In styles ranging from from classical to minimalist, tubs can be fixed to the wall, placed on a platform, inserted at floor level or positioned to stand alone. Available in a extensive range of materials, their shape can be symmetric, linear, curved or rounded to suit the style of the bathroom for which it is chosen.

Bisazza, an Italian company, produces a wide range of high-quality glass mosaic tiles, with which one can realize spectacular and luxury designs on the walls and even create whole bathtubs and showers.

Talisman with Giallo by Ann Sacks

Onzen by Ann Sacks

Maillot by Ann Sacks

Princess Yellow by Ann Sacks

Lansen by Ann Sacks

Jacuzzis

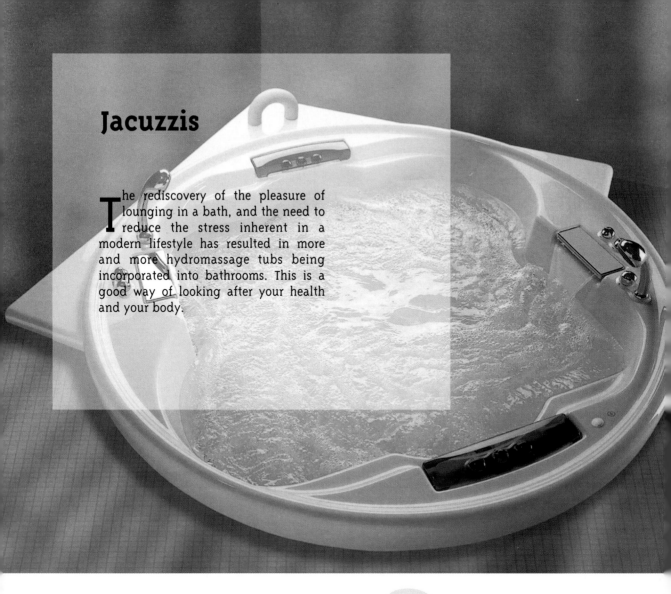

Jacuzzis

The rediscovery of the pleasure of lounging in a bath, and the need to reduce the stress inherent in a modern lifestyle has resulted in more and more hydromassage tubs being incorporated into bathrooms. This is a good way of looking after your health and your body.

Whirlpool: This is the original water massage technique. Jets of water mixed with air are in a fixed position, but their direction can be changed by manually adjusting the output jets. The effect is that of a massage at critical points of muscular tension, in general with a lymph drainage and vasodilatory action.

Airpool: A sophisticated system that uses the effect of blown air, as in natural "geysers". The gentle action on the bubbles envelops the whole body for a gentle full body massage.

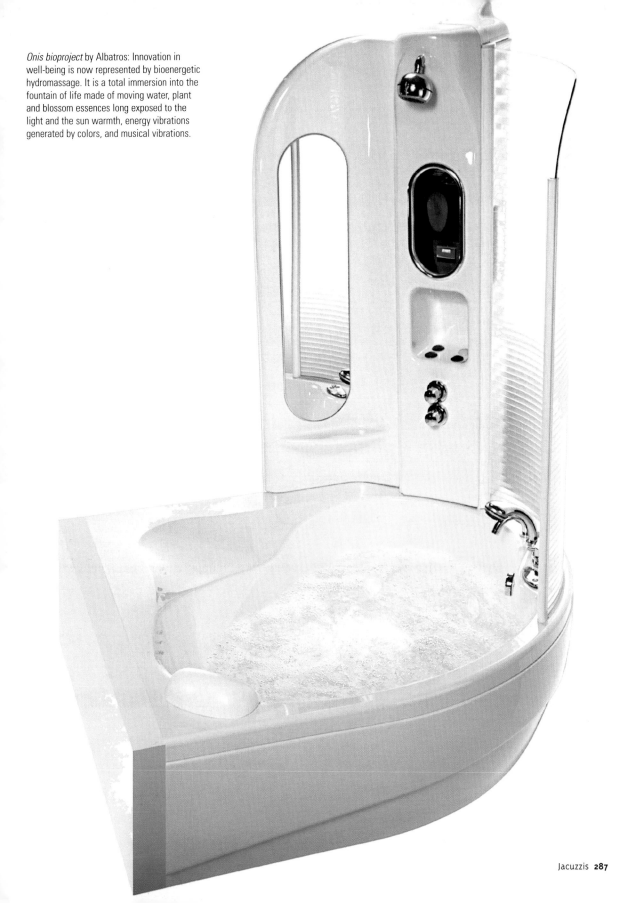

Onis bioproject by Albatros: Innovation in well-being is now represented by bioenergetic hydromassage. It is a total immersion into the fountain of life made of moving water, plant and blossom essences long exposed to the light and the sun warmth, energy vibrations generated by colors, and musical vibrations.

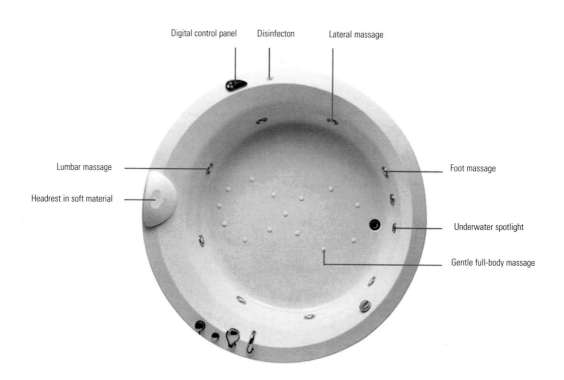

Digital control panel Disinfecton Lateral massage

Lumbar massage

Headrest in soft material

Foot massage

Underwater spotlight

Gentle full-body massage

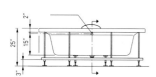

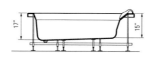

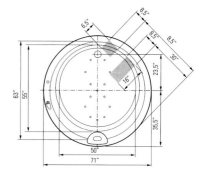

External Dimensions

Length/Width: ø 71 inches
Height: 25 inches

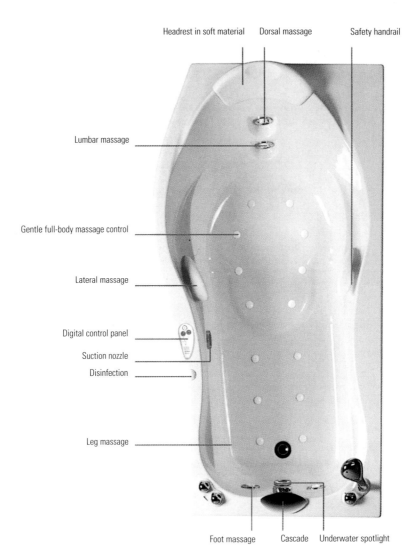

Headrest in soft material   Dorsal massage   Safety handrail

Lumbar massage

Gentle full-body massage control

Lateral massage

Digital control panel

Suction nozzle

Disinfection

Leg massage

Foot massage   Cascade   Underwater spotlight

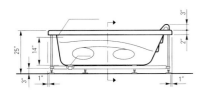

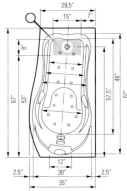

External Dimensions

Length: 67 inches
Width: 30/35 inches
Height: 25 inches

Jacuzzis

Rather than an occasional luxury, the Jacuzzi hydromassage can become a daily indulgence. That's the reason why Jacuzzi bathtubs are created to last a lifetime. An intelligent choice a Jacuzzi is also an excellent longterm investment.

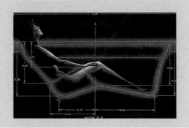

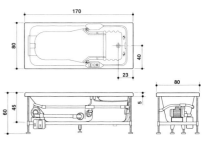

With the *Pulsar*, practical design is taken a step further. The hydrotherapy benefits provided by the whirlpool jets are intensified by innovative features.

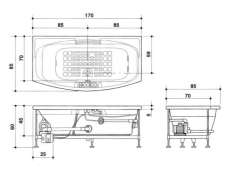

This spacious bath is part of the Jacuzzi® 5-jet hydromassage system, with contoured arm rests and an anti-slip base. With its compact size, the *Mya* suits smaller bathrooms model yet offers the comfort and luxury of a larger bath.

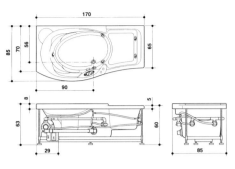

A whirlpool bath with an innovative design concept. On the lower level, the seat tilts to provide a comfortable position for an outstretched body-ideal massage. On the higher level, the seat is just right for taking a shower, or simply for having a foot bath.

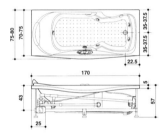

This intelligently designed unit combines pure shape with a concave/convex panel that creates a surprising amount of a space inside.

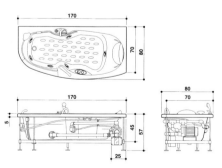

Just looking at, and stepping into the *Aulica* model makes you realize how an intelligent use of available space can result in optimum use without compromising the outside dimensions needed for all small bathrooms.

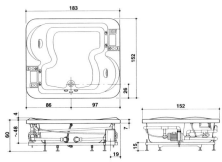

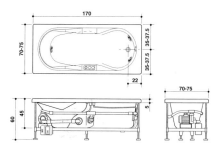

Aura offers a concealed toiletry compartment and two "Water Rainbow" cascades –one of which is connected to the hydromassage system and the other to the tap assembly supplied with the bath.

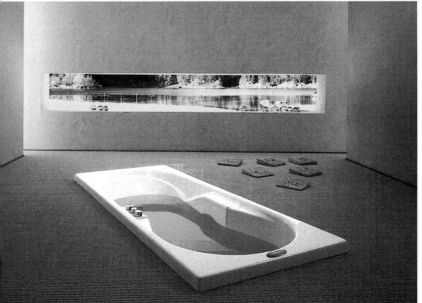

The enveloping curves and contours of the *Astra 75* have been designed to encourage the flow of water and enhance the hydromassage effect. Special attention has been given to the position of the controls to allow for installation of a shower screen.

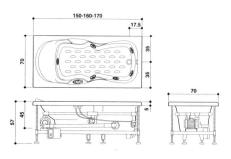

Harpa 150, 160 & 170: This tub has ergonomically designed backrest. Its compact size makes it ideal for small bathrooms.

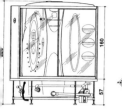

Flexa Twin is the perfect marriage of two instruments of pleasure with a true vocation for pampering: a whirpool bath and multi-function shower.

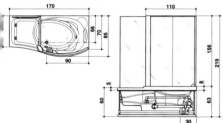

The *Twin Deck* is a revolutionary idea. An airy structure, the shower-area has been set in the widest part of the bath, which has an interior space of 32 x 43 inches. The enclosure contains all the bath and shower controls.

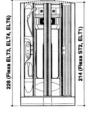

J-Dream Flexa 100x100: All the marvels of the *Flexa* collection, including the Turkish bath, are enclosed in a spacious shower stall.

Design by Philippe Starck for Duravit

Toilets and Bidets

Toilets and Bidets

Over the last few years the shap of toilets and bidets has changed enormously. Modern designs with straight or curved lines have become popular, along with cisterns fitted behind wall panels, but the classic English style —small, with elegant forms— has also remained in fashion.

Darling by Duravit

Previous page:
Serie 1930 by Duravit (above)
Bidet Victoria (below left) by Roca
Serie Meridian (below center and right) by Roca

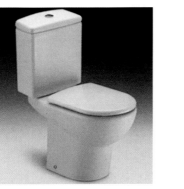

Serie Meridien by Roca (above)
Serie Victoria by Roca (left)

CMPX-519 by Franke

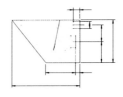

Happy D. by Duravit (above)
Mini Link by Flaminia (below)

Following page:
John & Mary by Rapsel, a wall-hung toilet and bidet in
highly polished stainless steel with solid beech seat
and cover.

Elements

Merdolino by Alessi
Previous page: *Dr. Kiss* by Alessi

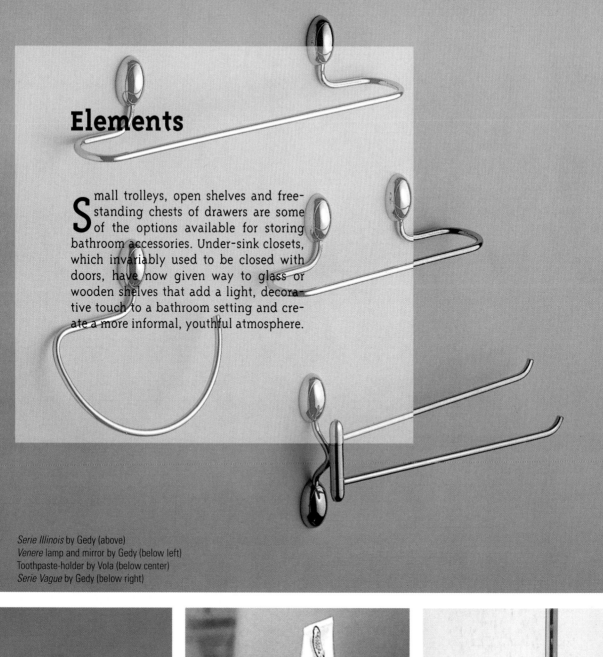

Elements

Small trolleys, open shelves and free-standing chests of drawers are some of the options available for storing bathroom accessories. Under-sink closets, which invariably used to be closed with doors, have now given way to glass or wooden shelves that add a light, decorative touch to a bathroom setting and create a more informal, youthful atmosphere.

Serie Illinois by Gedy (above)
Venere lamp and mirror by Gedy (below left)
Toothpaste-holder by Vola (below center)
Serie Vague by Gedy (below right)

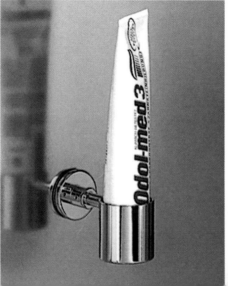

1. Cup and toothbrush holder by Vola
2. Magnetic soap holder by Vola
3. Towel ring by Vola
4. Toilet paper holder by Vola
5. Toiletbrush holder by Vola
6. Curved matte glass stool *Talo* by Altro
7. Built-in toilet flush by Vola
8. Toothbrush holder by Vola
9. Towel hook by Vola
10. Toilet paper holder by Vola
11. Soap holder by Vola

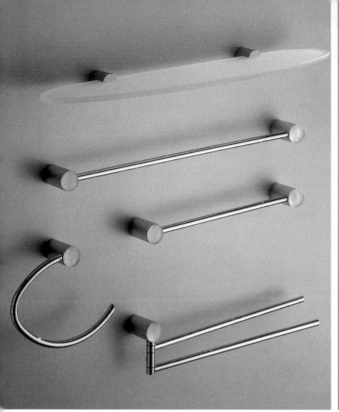

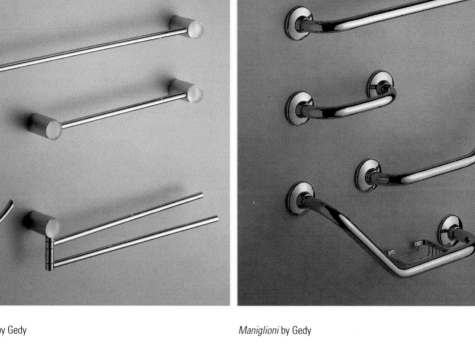

Serie Aura by Gedy

Maniglioni by Gedy

Serie Aura by Gedy

Serie Oregon by Gedy

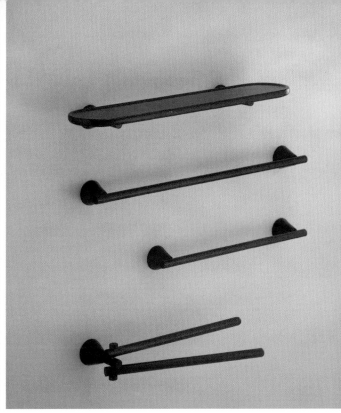

Serie 2500 Illinois by Gedy

Serie 2300 Oregon by Gedy

Serie 2700 Ascot by Gedy

Serie Mistral by Gedy

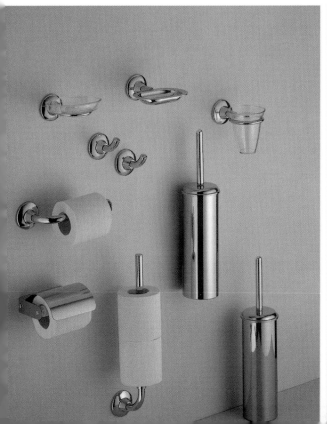

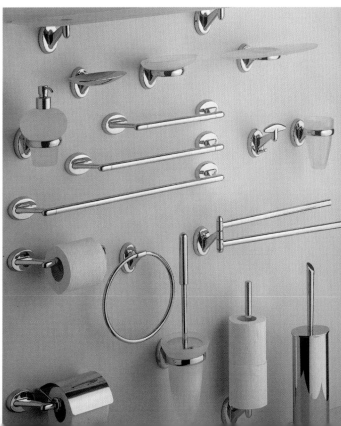

Oceanica by Gedy

Calla by Gedy

Fruit by Gedy

Oppla' by Gedy

Following page:
Toothbrush and soap holder
Flower and *Mexico* by Gedy

Serie Denise by Gedy

Hooks *un-dos-tres* by Gedy

Toiletbrush *Help* by Gedy

Serie Lara by Gedy

Toiletbrush *Strike* by Gedy

Details

Details

L inen towels, a few seashells or some
simple pictures on the wall —these are
just some of the details that can make
a bathroom more inviting and comfortable. Decorative elements must be chosen
in keeping with the style planned for the
bathroom, as well as whether or not the
elements are integrated into the bathroom. There is no need to overload the setting -one or two well— chosen details can
be enough to make a strong impact.

The small coloured tiles by Bizazza combine perfectly with natural materials just as with stainless steel (above and below).

Bath accessories by Ann Sacks

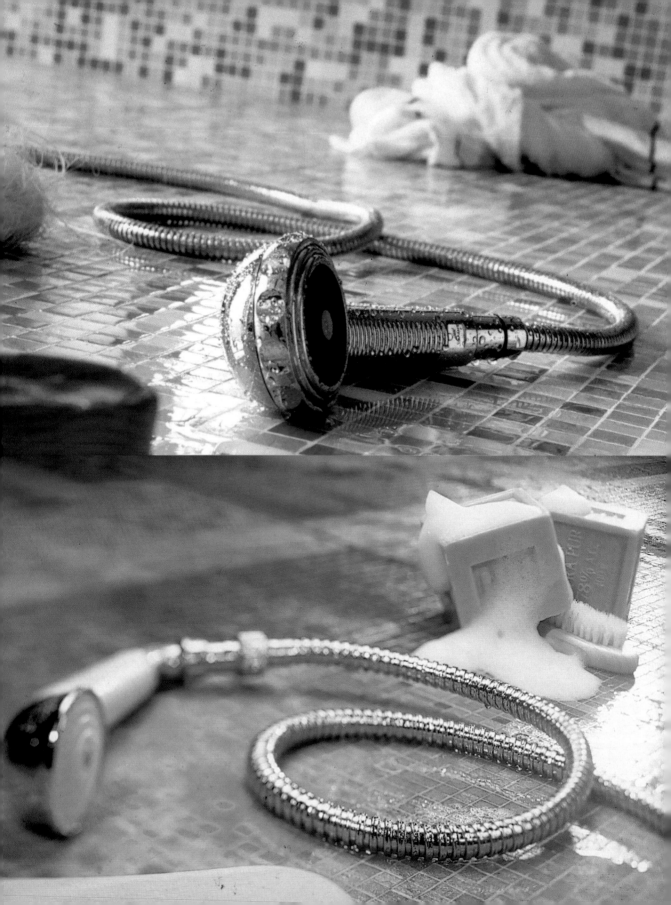

Princess Yellow lavatory by Ann Sacks

Previous page: *Kuo* round basin by Ann Sacks

Arch Spout lavatory set by Ann Sacks

One lavatory set by Ann Sacks

The Japanese Bath

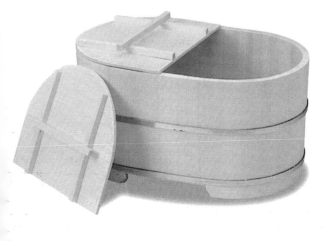

The Japanese Bath

One of the latest trends in bath design draws on the style and atmosphere of the traditional Japanese bath, usually built in hinoki (Japanese cypruss). This is a space designed for resting, taking it easy and eliminating stress. In fact, minimalism is a trend that grew out of the concept of the Japanese bath, which is stripped of all superfluous elements and overpowering decorative features.

"Colors of the walls should complement the warmth of the hinoki" Hinoki Soken

System Bath

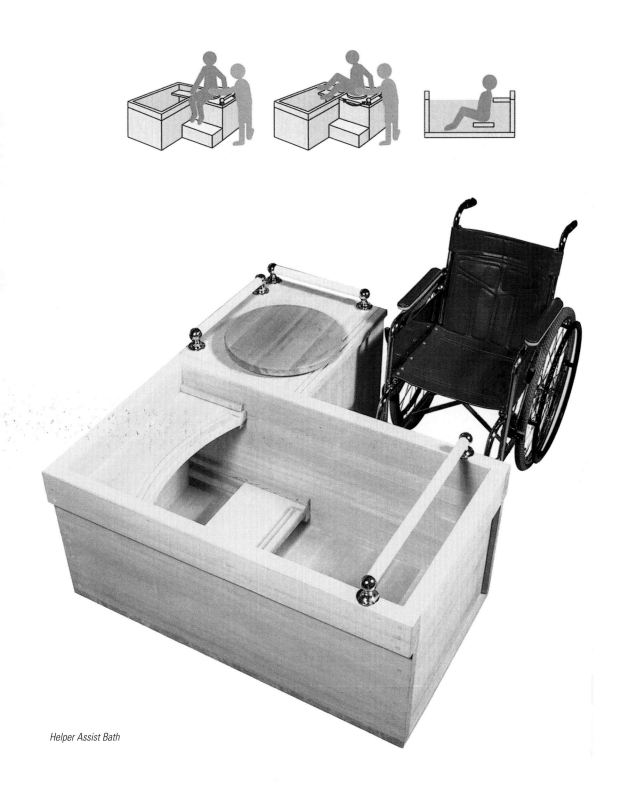

Helper Assist Bath

Directory

The publishers wish to thank the following companies for their valuable contribution:

Aiko Cucine	www.aiko.it aiko@aiko.it
Albatros	www.dominospa.com info@dominospa.com
Alessi	www.alessi.com info@alessi.com
Altro	www.altro.es altro@altro.es
Ann Sacks	www.annsacks.com
Arclinea	www.arclinea.it info@arclinea.it
ArtQuitect	artquitect@retemail.es
Bardelli	www.bardelli.it bardelli@bardelli.it
Binova	www.binova.com binova@binova.it
Bisazza	www.bisazza.it
Boffi	www.boffi.com info@boffi.com
Bulthaup	www.bulthaup.com
Candy	www.candy.it

Chalon	www.chalon.com
Daewoo	www.daewoo.com
Dornbracht	www.dornbracht.com
DuPont Corian	www.corian.com
Duravit	www.duravit.de info@duravit.de
Effeti Cucine	www.effeti.com info@effeti.ch
Electrolux	www.electrolux.com
Flaminia	www.ceramicaflaminia.it
Formica	www.formica-europe.com
Formica-Axiom	www.axiomworktops.com axiom.info@formica-europe.com
Franke	www.franke.com
Gabbianelli	www.gabbianelli.com gabbianelli@gabbianelli.com
Gaggenau	www.gaggenau.com
Gedy	www.gedy.com info@gedy.com
Hansgrohe	www.hansgrohe.de
Hinoki Soken	www.matrics.or.jp/hinokisoken/ kb698681@magic.matrics.or.jp

Jacob Delafon	www.jacobdelafon.com
Jacuzzi	www.jacuzzi.it
Leicht	www.leicht.com
Miele	www.miele.com
Nito	nitoarredamenti@tin.it
Poggenpohl	www.poggenpohl.de info@poggenpohl.de
Ramón Soler	www.ramonsoler.net
Rapsel	www.rapsel.it
Roca	www.roca.es
Rosières	www.rosieres.fr
Siematic	www.siematic.com
Trevi	www.trevishowers.co.uk
Veneta Cucine	www.venetacucine.com
Vola	www.vola.dk
Wellborn	www.wellborn.com jjordan@wellborn.com
Whirlpool	www.whirlpool.com
Zanussi	www.zanussi.com

Photo credits

© Montse Garriga   p. 86,111, 124,125,137,156 (below center), 226, 228, 229, 238, 239

© Vincent Leroux   p. 103

© Eugeni Pons   p. 131

© Hélène Binet   p.132 (above)

© Jonathan Pile   p. 132 (below right)

© Stella Rotger   p. 132 (below left), 280

© Georges Fessy   p. 235, 256 (above left)